The Story of Barnwood House Hospital

To Gordon
with grateful thanks
Richard

Printed by
Severn
Ashville Trading Estate
Bristol Road
Gloucester
GL2 5EU
www.severnprint.co.uk

Published by
Courtyard Books
The Homend Shopping Mall
32, The Homend
Ledbury
HR8 1BT
www.courtyardbooks.co.uk

Contents

Introduction

For the story of Barnwood House Hospital to be told requires us to travel many paths, stopping off along the way to visit places that help us understand the impact which the Hospital had, not only in Barnwood, but elsewhere.

Firstly, there is its history, from the time when the good people of Gloucester subscribed to the construction of a private mental Asylum around the early 1800s, right through to the ending of Barnwood Trust's involvement in Barnwood in 2022. The first part of this book tells that story chronologically.

The second part tells the story of how the Hospital operated, its ethos, and the people that made it function so successfully.

The third part is called the Barnwood House Estate. After some 100 years in Barnwood, the Hospital owned a considerable amount of land to the south of the main building, many peripheral, or satellite buildings, as well as a large swathe of land to the north of Barnwood Road. This section shows how the estate developed over the years and what happened to the land. Today, much of it is occupied by industrial units or the houses of the Abbeydale and Abbeymead developments.

Lastly there is a section on patients, some statistics, and a few life stories.

Some parts of this story run in parallel, especially around the closure of the main building, the development at Manor Gardens, and the development of the Hospital's lands. There is therefore some duplication where the same story is told in different ways reflecting where it fits into the history.

Today the body that was known during some of the Hospital's lifetime as The Barnwood House Trust is now known as Barnwood Trust. This body is a very different entity with a very different set of objectives to that which managed Barnwood House Hospital.

Throughout this book the terms, Management Committee, 'Hospital Trust' or where the context is obvious, 'Trust', are used to refer to the early overarching management of the Hospital, and where relevant, 'Barnwood Trust' to refer to the modern organisation whose heritage is Barnwood House Hospital.

The phrase 'mental asylum' is not used these days and may give offence to some. However, this was used by the Hospital at various times to describe itself, and so, where appropriate, and to maintain historical accuracy, this term has been used to refer to the Hospital.

This book is based on a very comprehensive study which I have written on the Hospital, and many facts come from two detailed articles written by people who worked there and knew the Hospital well, its secretary during the early years Tom Gale, and following him, Bill Church. Their style of prose is different from mine and stands out where I have used their text without edits.

Much has also been gleaned from the deposition of the Hospital's records in The Gloucestershire Archives (ref: D3725) and I am grateful to both them and The Barnwood Trust for permissions to access and use this material.

I have intentionally not peppered this book with references as it is meant to be read without much interruption. But where I felt some amplification was needed there are footnotes.

One reason for this book is that whenever my good friend and colleague, Brain McBurnie and I gave a talk on the Hospital there would always be a great deal of interest and comment.

In our books on Barnwood (Tales; More Tales; and Even More Tales) those chapters on the Hospital were read with interest. If you have read these books, some sections in this one will be familiar as several of those articles have been reproduced here.

Each section has its own colour for the headings. This should help navigate through the book.

This is a big book with a lot of information and detail. I have tried to keep the sections in readable bites so that the reader does not get overwhelmed.

Dr. Frederick Needham, one of the Head Doctors of the Hospital, did much to ensure that the Hospital's buildings were designed to enhance the wellbeing of its patients and to increase the chances of their recovery.

In the annual report of 1891, he stated that he wanted the Hospital to be a "**Home from Home**" for his patients. A phrase which I felt summed up the ethos of the Hospital and therefore a suitable title for a book on its history.

Richard Auckland
October 2022

The Desire for a Mental Asylum

One consequence of the dissolution of the monasteries in the middle of the 16th century was the resultant loss of hospitals and the skills to maintain them. Over the subsequent years the care of those unwell, either physically or mentally, degenerated, became crude and often inhumane.

For those suffering with mental problems and who could afford to pay, care was obtainable either in their own homes or in the houses of physicians. But those unable to fend for themselves were often seen as a burden.

Many were sent either to poor houses or placed in prison, neither of which were equipped to treat or care for such inmates. Often the conditions in which they lived were barbaric.

In 1774 an Act of Parliament for the regulating and licensing of private 'madhouses' was passed replacing the Poor Law Act of 1601. Also, in that year the Justices Commitment Act affecting the care of the insane by parishes was passed. This Act provided that the Justices could, by warrant, direct constables, churchwardens, and overseers of the poor to cause insane persons to be apprehended and locked up in a secure place.

This in effect meant incarceration in the local gaol with mechanical restraint, often in the form of chains.

Even in 1788, the sovereign King George III, during his periods of insanity was encased in a machine, leaving no liberty of movement, and chained to a staple, so the treatment of the insane sovereign was like that of the pauper, even if the surroundings were more congenial. [1]

By 1800 most large cities possessed infirmaries, and a few of the more enlightened cities had asylums in addition. However, it was not until the

---

[1] Much of this early history is based on an article written by Ann Bailey – Transactions of the BGAS 1971, Vol. 90, p p 178-191

mid-18th and early 19th centuries that hospitals were being opened in and around Gloucester. The most important, the Gloucester Infirmary, which was a subscription hospital in lower Southgate Street, opened about 1755.

Many of the hospitals in and around Gloucester were established by private initiatives, reflecting the altruistic attitudes of the middle and upper classes who were benefitting from the commercial growth of Gloucester around this time.

Still, the treatment of mental patients, although now predominantly placed in medical hospitals, was in many cases not appropriate for their specific needs and care.

The idea of an asylum in Gloucester was first promoted at an Infirmary weekly meeting in January 1792 when it was proposed that one should be added to the existing complex of infirmary buildings. After discussions it was felt that however great the need, funds were not available for these additions to the existing establishment.

It was not until July 1793 that the matter was raised again when, at an Infirmary meeting, it was proposed that a separate asylum should be set up in Gloucester.

Thus, in September 1793, largely because of the influence of Sir George Paul, it was resolved: -

> That a 'General Hospital of Insane Persons' should be established.

> That the means of supporting the expenses of the establishment should be by payments from patients.

> That the President, Vice President, and Governors of the Gloucester Infirmary, with well-wishers, were to solicit contributions for the erection of the buildings.

They adopted a scheme of finance for its operation that was created by Sir George Paul[2], who modelled it principally on that operating at the Asylum in York.[3]

Funding would be by payments from patients, and it would cater for three classes of patients: the wealthy, the poor on parochial relief, and the poor not on relief. Payments from the poor not on relief were subsidised by funds derived from surplus payments by wealthy patients, benefactions, and legacies.

So, the governors of the Gloucester Infirmary opened a subscription whose sole purpose was to fund the building of an independent lunatic asylum in Gloucester.

Initially, £1,000 was subscribed, and as funds increased rapidly to £2,923, it was thought necessary to call a primary general meeting of the subscribers. At this meeting, held on the 16th of January 1794, subscribers were requested to pay in their subscriptions and means of promoting subscriptions were discussed. A treasurer, secretary and committee were appointed, and a declaration was made to the effect that

> 'The Gloucester Lunatic Asylum was proposed to be a general establishment for the reception of all persons offered for admission who should be adjudged to labour under an unsound state of mind'.

---

[2] Sir George Onesiphorus Paul, 2nd Baronet (1746–1820) was a Gloucestershire born prison reformer and philanthropist.

[3] The York Asylum, opened in 1777, was built with public subscriptions and was maintained by payments from patients and friends. However, it was discovered that some patients were held in terrible squalor. Indeed the conditions at the asylum were the stimulus for the foundation in 1796 of 'The Retreat' at York which became world renowned for its pioneering treatment of the mentally ill, pioneering the so-called "moral treatment" that became a behaviour model for asylums around the world.
The Hospital, in its early days, was visited by staff from the Retreat, and it certainly followed the 'moral treatment ethos promoted by them.

This project was not to interfere with infirmary funds, nor to be assisted by annual subscriptions, the patients must be maintained by payment from friends or the parishes to which they belonged.

Many notable and important dignitaries were amongst the subscribers, amongst them the Baronet Sir John Guise, Sir George Paul, William Hyett MP., George Talbot, Thomas Mee, Sir Thomas Crawley-Bovey, and the Bishop of Gloucester.

The funds at that time were insufficient for building to start, however the following year the subscribers purchased an Inn and two houses south of the Infirmary as an intended site for their Asylum.

Initially, the Subscribers struggled to raise sufficient funds for their enterprise, but by 1811 when the funds stood at £8,250, they had sufficient to buy some eight acres of land at Wotton on the outskirts of Gloucester for their Asylum, and an architect was engaged.

Funds were increased, when in 1813, they sold their site in Southgate Street to the Infirmary. But the subscribers still lacked sufficient funds to build and run an Asylum on their site in Wotton.

In 1806, the Sheriff of Gloucestershire, Sir George Paul addressed a letter to the Secretary of State about criminal and pauper lunatics. This led to the setting up of a select committee "to enquire into the state of criminal and pauper lunatics in England, the laws relating there to".

As a result, in 1808 the first 'County Asylum Act' [4] was passed, and it was the terms of this act that caused the radical change in ideas of how the Gloucester Asylum should be financed.

---

[4] Also known as the 'Lunatic, Paupers or Criminals Act (48 Geo III c.96)' This act, partly experimental in nature, was also permissive.
It was amended three times, the last occasion being 1819 and it was superseded in 1828 by a further County Asylum Act.

This Act allowed Justices to raise a county rate for the purpose of building an asylum and could mortgage the rate for a period not exceeding fourteen years. An appeal for voluntary contributions could also be made.

Passing this Act, meant that the original scheme envisaged by the subscribers needed to be considerably modified.

On the 26th of August 1812 at a meeting of the subscribers, it was decided that, as the subscriptions of £10,946 14s. 6d. were insufficient to carry out the resolutions of 14th July 1794 regarding the building of an asylum, these were to be rescinded. It was resolved instead "that it appears no longer necessary or expedient to provide a place of reception for lunatics who are dependent on parish relief, but to be advisable to unite with the County". In simple terms, this meant that both the County and City could now raise money from the rates for building an asylum and that the Subscribers who wanted to run a private Asylum could negotiate with these bodies.

At a further meeting on 9th October 1812 the Subscribers appointed representatives to negotiate with the Magistrates. These deliberations resulted in the following proposals.

'Firstly, that both the County and City Magistrates and subscribers should proceed immediately to build an asylum'.

'Secondly, that the necessary expenses of providing the building, fittings, repairs, and maintenance should be defrayed by the parties. The county was to pay eleven parts of the building and maintenance costs, the city one, and the subscribers eight'.

In 1813, the three parties agreed to this union to provide both private accommodation for the wealthy who could afford it, and accommodation for paupers.

The Hospital was to be known as Wotton Lawn Asylum

Wotton Lawn Asylum

Known in recent times as Horton Road Hospital, it closed in 1988, and subsequently, in 2005, was converted into domestic accommodation.

The building of the asylum in Horton Road, Wotton, just within the city boundary, began in 1814 to a plan by William Stark of Edinburgh, modified by John Wheeler. They were chosen solely on account of their experience and supposed skill in constructing such edifices. Yet the form chosen was a crescent – the most expensive and the worst for supervision that could have been adopted. The rooms which were built in the basement expressly for patient's sleeping apartments were found suitable only for cellars and storerooms. Very little of the original building could be made use of for the accommodation of patients.

Completion was delayed, caused mainly by financial problems encountered by the subscribers.

Wotton Asylum was eventually opened in 1823. Built of brick and stucco, its central feature was a crescent of three storeys with its principal elevation facing east. [5]

North, south, and west wings of two storeys were connected to the crescent by day rooms. The crescent contained accommodation for 24 wealthy patients and their servants and the wings for 60 paupers and 26 charity patients. There were detached wards for noisy and violent patients.

The Asylum was governed by a committee consisting of County magistrates. City magistrates and the Subscribers.
The subscribers also maintained a charity to reduce the charges on poor patients not on parochial relief.

---

[5] Much of this section is from 'The History of Horton Road and Coney Hill Hospitals' by Ian Hollingsbee (used with his permission).

Wotton Lawn c1900.

For this enterprise to be successful the early establishment of a smooth and sound relationship needed to be established between all the parties concerned, with scrupulous observance by all. Sadly, records show that there was an element of friction.

From the outset, the Hospital's management was beset with problems, particularly the need of both the County and City to house an increasing number of poor, and the subscribers' lack of funds.

In 1828 Samuel Hitch was appointed the resident medical superintendent.

Aged just 28 on appointment, Samuel Hitch could be considered the innovative forerunner of the long line of Superintendents who would influence the care that Barnwood House Hospital became well known for.

Under his leadership, Wotton Lawn Asylum prospered over the coming years. He was described as an able, bustling, intelligent man, short in stature and with red hair. He was well educated, and in 1841 he became the principal founder of the Royal Medico-Psychological Association.

Samuel Hitch quickly developed a reputation in the treatment of his patients. He was particularly interested in Moral Insanity, General Paralysis of the Insane, and the recovery rate in Asylums. Certainly, he was keen to try new treatments, but his innovation of giving his patients trial leave prior to discharge was highly criticized by the Commissioners in Lunacy[6] who stated that it was 'contrary to law'.

In the first five years of his tenure at Horton Road, there were 252 admissions and an amazing 56% of these patients were discharged as 'recovered'. This is said to have been the highest recovery rate in the country.

Hitch trusted his patients 'to an extent not generally believed possible'. He always took the patient's word, and he allowed at least 20 percent of his patients to be under no restrictions to their movements. They were

---

[6] The Commissioners in Lunacy were a public body established by the Lunacy Act 1845 to oversee asylums and the welfare of mentally ill people in England and Wales.

reported to have been allowed to attend the church in town unescorted or in self-supporting

He was just as keen to adopt innovations and progressive ideas from other asylums. By 1841, and despite opposition from the visiting Justices, he had abandoned the use of restraint groups.

That year may well have been the first instance of a female nurse working with male patients. The wife of a charge attendant was employed on a male refractory ward as Hitch's motive was to encourage a 'gentler atmosphere on the ward'.

Nurses exercising patients on the lawns beside the chapel

The Hospital continued to adopt new ideas which benefited the patients. The absence of mechanical restraint resulted in patients being better behaved. Neary half the patients were allowed to sleep in dormitories of four to sixteen beds rather than a separate cell for each patient.

Another remarkable innovation was the introduction of a 'self-governing' group of patients. These patients worked in the gardens and lived in a separate building on their own, which was said to have been outside the asylum walls. These patients were under the supervision of the head gardener who lived at some distance from them, and they were free to come and go as they so wished.

These privileges were, however, only extended to the better class of patient and not to the Charitable or Pauper patients.

The exercising grounds, formerly the scenes of occasional riot and confusion were now laid out as vegetable and flower gardens.

Dances, concerts where patients took part in the singing, parties and excursions were promoted.

In 1847, Hitch severed his connexion with the asylum and opened a private Mental Institution at Sandywell Park, Dowdeswell, near Cheltenham.

His legacy was to continue many years later in the ethos of Barnwood House Hospital.

By 1855 the number of pauper patients had risen to 310. To accommodate this growing number of patients, large new wings for paupers were opened both in 1852 and 1855.

This growth in the numbers of public patients put a strain on the Subscribers and their private patients. Both the numbers of private patients and the surplus of funds from their fees were lower than had been envisaged. Because of lack of space the areas originally build for use by private patients were becoming occupied by public patients, much to the discomfort of the Subscribers and their private patients.

There were now two standards of care operating in close proximity, a source of some friction. In short, the building was not being used in the way that the Subscribers had envisaged. Another source of friction was that the hospital's administration was failing to satisfy the Subscribers that the excess funds from the wealthy patients were being used solely for the remainder of the private patients' benefit.

It was becoming clear that the joint venture between County and City and the Subscribers was not beneficial to either side. In 1843, after some protracted negotiations and a resort to litigation, the part of the building owned by the Subscribers was purchased by the County and City in order to accommodate the growing numbers of their patients.

The implications of this settlement hastened the decision of both the County and City to terminate the union which began in 1813 but which was now not satisfactory to any of the parties.

A deed was agreed, the Subscribers were not only given £13,000 payment for releasing all their remaining property, rights and interest in the building but were also given an additional sum, being the payments of wealthy patients "credited in error". The admission of this financial error must have given the Subscribers much satisfaction.

So, in 1856 the union between County, City, and Subscribers was finally dissolved. The County and City set about converting the building for the exclusive use of paupers. The Wotton Asylum then became known as The County Asylum.

The private patients were rehoused by the Subscribers. Nine of the charity patients were supported in a private asylum in Fairford.

The subscribers were now without a suitable building and looking for a new home.

A Gentleman's Residence

Barnwood House, sited on the south side of the Turnpike Road[7] from Gloucester to Cirencester, was built as a gentleman's residence sometime during the first five years of the nineteenth century. It was a square block of three storeys with two full-height bays, facing an extensive garden to the south, with a service wing to the west and a semi-circular drive at the front.

It was built by Robert Morris of nearby Barnwood Court, a partner in the Gloucester bank of Turner and Morris and MP for Gloucester from 1805 to 1816. It is unlikely that Morris built the house for his own use as he had recently undertaken considerable improvements to the Court, and so it is possible that it was intended for his son Robert. However, Robert junior set up home in Cheltenham where he ran a branch of the bank and probably never lived in this house.

Sir Charles Hotham then purchased the House, around 1804.

As well as buying the land immediately associated with the house, Sir Charles also purchased neighbouring properties fronting on to the turnpike road, together with the field between those properties and the Wotton Brook and some fields to the south of the brook.

One difficulty was that a public footpath ran across the field close behind his house. In 1810, Sir Charles managed to get this right of way diverted on to neighbouring roads and off his lands.

Sir Charles died at Barnwood House on the 18th of July 1811 at the age of 45.

In the following year the house was put up for sale with 48 acres of land.

_____

[7] Barnwood Road was previously called London Road or the Turnpike Road.

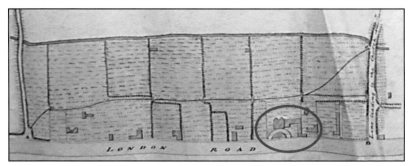

This map of 1810 shows Sir Charles' House (circled) fronting London Road, and the footpath running between Upton Lane on the left and Church Lane on the right.

The next occupants of Barnwood House were the Walters Family. David Walters purchased Barnwood House and its grounds in 1813.

In 1819 when David's son, James Woodbridge Walters, married Sarah Adams from Painswick House, they set up home together at Barnwood House.[8]

The house was described as 'beautifully situated on a lawn, fronting to the south, commanding extensive and highly diversified views of the adjacent country'. The property included a greenhouse and a kitchen garden which was 'surrounded with lofty walls well clothed with the choicest fruit trees'. David Walters lived in the house until his death on 6 May 1833, when it then became the home of his son, James.

Either David or James had added wings to the original house by the time of the Tithe Survey in 1838. The lawn and garden extended about 50 yards behind the house, and then there was a pasture sloping down to the Wotton Brook, which was dammed to form a small lake.

---

[8] This marriage and their residence in Barnwood House would, some years later, influence the choice by the subscribers to purchase this house for their Asylum in Barnwood. The Chairman of the Subscribers at that time was William Henry Hyett, previously known as William Adams, the brother of Sarah Adams. Both lived at Painswick House.

The Tithe Map shows trees to the east and west of the pasture, framing the view from the house which included two distant spinnies. There was also a plantation of trees on the north side of the main road. To the east of the house were two cottages, a walled kitchen garden and an orchard sloping down to the brook. Both father and son had added land to the estate on both sides of the main road, and by 1838 the total area was 719 acres.

As well as being a director of the County of Gloucester Bank, James Woodbridge Walters also became prominent in public life. He was a captain in the volunteer militia, a Justice of the Peace and, in 1841, Sheriff of Gloucestershire.

It seems, however, that his pretensions were rather greater than his resources, and when he died in 1852, he was heavily in debt.

He had arranged for the bank to settle all his debts in exchange for taking over his property, but the bank soon found that the debts considerably exceeded the value of the estate. Walters owed £75K but the estate was estimated to be only worth just over £52K. The Bank's directors did not acknowledge this as a bad debt until their annual report of 1868.

By his death, Walters owned most of the land either side of the main road running through Barnwood, from the railway line eastwards to the border with Hucclecote.

This extensive Barnwood Estate was put on the market on Tuesday the 8th of November 1853. Comprising over 670 acres which were divided into 40 Lots; the sales bill listed several substantial residences, farms, and farm buildings, 2 corn (maybe gin) mills, several dwelling houses, and numerous cottages.

However, the high expectations and unrealistic pricing meant that the estate did not sell in its entirety at first offering, instead it was sold off piecemeal, parts still being offered by the bank as late as March 1867.

Establishing the Hospital in Barnwood

In 1856, having agreed the separation from their joint venture at Wotton Asylum in Horton Road, the Committee of Subscribers with William Henry Hyett as its chairman, met frequently to plan the future of their enterprise. Most likely, the committee were unable to move until their ties with the Hospital in Horton Road were completely severed and their finances were clearly understood. Once they had plenary powers and available capital with more donations and subscriptions in prospect they could proceed with the purchase of a suitable property.

W. H. Hyett and his fellow committee must have known well before they moved out of Horton Road the type and location of property that would suit their needs.

William Henry Hyett
First Chairman of Barnwood
House Hospital 1860 - 1862

Hyett's family name was Adams
He changed his surname in 1813, after being left the estates of Benjamin Hyett and subsequently resided at Painswick House, in Gloucestershire.
His sister, Sarah Adams, had married James Woodbridge Walters, so Hyett would have known Barnwood House and grounds when the couple moved there around 1833.

James Walters' death in 1853 and the subsequent difficulty the bank had of disposing of the estate would have been well known to the subscribers as they sought a new home around 1856. At this time, parts of this estate had still not been sold and so the subscribers decided that they would purchase it as it would be an ideal place in which to set up and develop their asylum.

In May 1857, the subscribers offered to purchase Barnwood House and some of the surrounding ground, but it was not until February 1858, some eight months after their initial offer, possibly reflecting the complexity of the transaction, that the sale was completed.

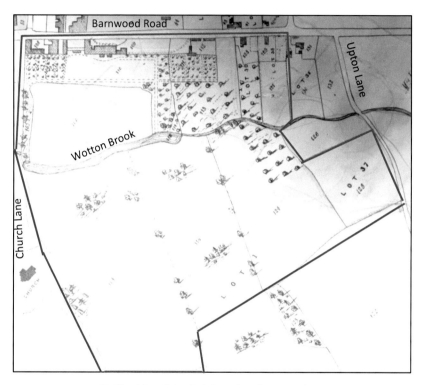

Outlined in red is what the subscribers purchased

They purchased for £7,800 the house and some of its grounds and three other lots, adjacent to each other alongside the man road to the east of the House. In total, just over 48 acres.

The house was a relatively small early 19th-century villa of stuccoed brick with a symmetrical three-story garden front and two-story wings either side.

Whilst the first floor had 2 bed chambers and dressing rooms, the top (second) floor of the main house had 4 bedrooms and a dressing room.

The two 2-story wings were different sizes. The first floor of the east wing had 2 bedrooms with a water closet, whilst the west wing was bigger, the first floor having 3 bedrooms, 2 servant's rooms, and a 'secondary staircase'.

The ground floors of the main building and that of the east wing were listed as having a hall, dining room, drawing room, library, and water closet. The west wing was being used for servants and their utilities, for its description included a housekeeper's room, storeroom, butler's pantry, servant's hall, china closet, kitchen, and scullery with a 'man's room' over.
There was, as one would expect, a good wine and beer cellar.

Outside, the plot had numerous outhouses, a knife house, cool larder, coal house, brew house – with laundry over, dairy, gardener's room – with a bedroom over.

The carriage yard was serviced with both a 5-stall stable, and a 3-stall stable, saddle room, 2 coach houses, 3 loose boxes, and a hay room.

The farmyard comprised a granary, stable, 3 loose boxes, a shed for cows, and cattle sheds.

There were two cottages, occupied by tenants. These were in the north-western corner of the land, facing the main road.

A conservatory with a productive kitchen garden and orchard completed the purchase.

Once the sale was complete, permission was sought, and obtained, from the Home Secretary for the establishment of a private asylum in Barnwood.

Plans for the conversion of the House and its two wings were drawn up by the architect Walter B Wood,[9] and the lessons learned from the mistakes in the building at Horton Road were applied. The firm of Fulljames and Waller[10] then converted the property into a hospital suitable for private patients. Over £7,000 was spent on converting the building and grounds.

Eighteen months after the purchase, on the 12th of November 1859, an advertisement was placed in the Gloucester Journal announcing the opening of Barnwood House 'a public institution for private patients'.

It asked for subscription or donation, envisaging that the institution would become self-supporting within five years.

With the publication of a prospectus, and accompanying publicity; considerable interest was aroused, and substantial contributions were received.

Much work had been done to convert the building into a suitable hospital. The main house was converted to a residence for the Medical Superintendent with some offices and communal rooms on the ground floor.

---

[9] Wood was a notable Barnwood resident and architect who initially worked for Fulljames and Waller. He became the Hospital's architect as it grew and changed over the subsequent years.

He lived as a child at Sandywell Park, the Asylum Run by Samuel Hitch, the early and innovative Head of Wotton Asylum, and where his father was a general practitioner. Walter's father-in-law became the first Superintendent of Barnwood House Hospital.

[10] F. S. Waller was the son in Law of Samuel Hitch. He spent some time living in, and subsequently managing Hitch's Hospital, Sandywell Park at Dowdeswell, so knew the requirements for a well-functioning hospital.

The service buildings in the grounds to the west, and the northern part of the west wing were pulled down. The stucco was removed from both wings, they were raised by the addition of a third storey and extended symmetrically on either side to provide accommodation for about 70 patients. These wings ended in towers which housed the Hospital's water tanks.

The west wing, the Church Lane end, was to house male patients while the east was for female patients.

All rooms had open fireplaces and were also warmed by hot water piping, which was supplied by boilers in the basement. These boilers were coal fired for, at that time, a gas supply had not been laid to the building.

Water was obtained from the Wotton Brook which ran through the grounds. Two hydraulic rams installed at the weir pumped this water up to the two water tanks housed at the top of the towers at either end of the accommodation wings.

Sewerage was piped to two cesspits which were some distance north of the Hospital, across the Barnwood Road. These pits may well have been open, for in 1892 the land around these was becoming saturated and chemical filtration was installed in order to improve the situation.

The Hospital installed flushing toilets, a very modern facility for the time.

The gardens were extended down to the brook with gravel walks and additional trees and shrubs. The walled kitchen garden was reserved as an airing ground for the ladies, and a separate area was enclosed with a paling as "a court for the more excited gentlemen patients". A bridge was built near to the weir so that patients could follow a gravel walk around the field beyond the brook, returning via an existing bridge further east. The route of this walk, known as the Ladies' Mile, was marked by a line of trees. How much of all this was complete by the opening is not clear, but certainly within a few years this reflected the Hospital's grounds and its amenities.

In January 1860 Barnwood House Hospital was almost ready to receive patients, the first on the 6th of January, which was recorded as the official opening date.

Dr Alfred J Wood was its first Superintendent, and his wife, Frances, was Matron.

As a couple they would go on to serve the Hospital for the next fourteen years. Their starting salary was £300 plus board and lodging.

Male attendants were paid £24. 14s. 8d and female £7. 19s. 4d. a quarter.

Patients of both sexes ate in the communal dining room in the main building, along with the Medical Superintendent and Matron. This was a requirement of the early rules, indicating the importance of a family like atmosphere.

During the early months, the admissions were few, partially due to the Hospital not being fully equipped.

By 11 August 1860, 14 patients had been received and by the end of the year 25 patients had been admitted, 11 of whom left having recovered.

The first year was difficult financially, income from patients was less than one half of the cost of their keep. There was still considerable expenditure on buildings, furniture, and grounds. This had, however, been anticipated by the Committee.

The census of 1861, taken in March of that year, records those living there were the Wood family, seven female patients, twelve male patients, three male attendants, three female nurses, a cook, kitchen maid, and three housemaids.

The second year saw a rise in admissions and income, which continued for the next two years, so that by the end of the fourth-year income from patients equalled the cost of their keep.

This was a turning point for the Hospital, and an indication that the statement that the Committee had made "that the Hospital would be self-supporting within five years" would be met.

It was now time for a change of leadership.

In 1862, William Hyett stepped down as Chairman, to be replaced by his son in law, Sebastian Stewart Dickinson M.P.

Dickinson took over at a good time for the Hospital, for in the years that followed there was a comfortable financial surplus, thus freeing the Hospital from the subscriptions and donations required at the start. This now enabled the Hospital to plan for amenities on a long-term basis.

It was said of Dickinson that "It is impossible to over-estimate the value of his services. He had a wonderful memory for detail and an inexhaustible capacity for concentrated

S. S. Dickinson.

work. His knowledge of the patients was most extensive, he occasionally entertained them at his own home and many of them felt they possessed in him a friend".

A railing or fence was erected along Church Lane which was "most beneficial in preventing communication with persons on the other side both by attendants and patients."

By 1864 the Hospital, with 60 patients, was full.

Over the following years the accommodation wings were altered and extended with new buildings being added in the late 19th and early 20th century.

In 1866 night-nursing was introduced. It can only be assumed that up to then, ministration to patients during the night was ad-hoc.

This early view of the southern aspect of the Hospital shows the central block
with the two three-storied wings either side.

In 1869 a chapel, designed by F. S. Waller was built in the grounds south
of the Wotton Brook. It was rebuilt in 1887 when a south aisle and vestry
were added.

In 1880, the Hospital's Chaplain was the Reverend C Naylor, who was the
highly regarded Headmaster of the Crypt School in Gloucester.

On average there were 80 attendees at the services. It was a requirement
that staff attended these reflecting, perhaps, the Christian ethos of the
Hospital.

The Rebuilt Hospital Chapel

Sadly, on the 23rd of August 1878 at the age of 63, having spent sixteen years as the Hospital's chairman, Sebastian Dickinson died.

The Hospital's next chairman was William Ancrum.
He was a most experienced retired naval surgeon, who lived in St Leonards Court, Upton St Leonards, not far from the Hospital.

He continued the expansion of the Hospital, something much needed, for due to its success, there were insufficient beds and facilities for those who wished to be treated there.

In 1877 the Hospital had an 'unusually prosperous' year and a Christmas bonus was given to the staff, depending upon their wage and length of service. 22 people were named.
This ranged from £1 for the 17-year-old pantry boy William Bennett to £100 for Doctor Needham and £50 for his wife.

In 1878 the ladies' wing was extended to the east and a southern facing conservatory was planned. The male wing needed improving with more day rooms.

More land was purchased on the northern side of the road to bring the total to 213 acres.[11] Drainage continued to be discharged there for eventual use as fertiliser for the fields.

A large and external laundry was now needed to replace the one in the underground passageway below the Hospital. It was to be built on this newly acquired land.

In 1880, admissions were limited due to the Hospital being 'overcrowded' with forty patients having to be refused for lack of space. A recovery rate of 46%, though "more than satisfactory" did not reduce patient numbers sufficiently to overcome this situation.

The 1881 census recorded 63 male patients and 82 females resident in the Hospital at that time. The oldest of whom was 91, the youngest, 18. There were 98 patients recorded as 'living on own means' – 80 females 18 males. Indicating that over half the patients were wealthy, and the majority of them were female. There were also clergymen, schoolmasters, farmers, students, solicitors, a retired governess, and a retired hospital nurse, indicating the wide range of patients the Hospital treated.

By this time, the Hospital was treating daily, on average, some 110 patients. This created a surplus of £4,482, which was used to increase the comfort of the patients by extending the living quarters and by creating a cricket ground alongside the chapel.

This surplus also benefited those who could not afford treatment. Always a source of concern to the committee was the balance between those who could pay and those who could not.

---

[11] There must have been significant, unrecorded, purchases of land in the 20 or so years previously as the initial purchase was only 43 acres.

In 1888, at the High Court, the Hospital management lost their hard-fought battle for Schedule D Tax exemption[12], on the grounds that the Hospital was self-sustaining and did not rely on charitable donations. This would have not helped the Hospital's finances.

Ancrum gave much to the Hospital during the seventeen years he served as chairman, however ill health forced him to retire in 1895, and the last three years of his life were spent at the family home. He died on the 9th of October 1898. The Annual Report of 1899 stated that "During the eventful period of his chairmanship, the Hospital, grew from a small institution to one of the most successful of its kind in the land".

---

[12] This was to do with the profits and losses from selling and buying capital. it

Into the Twentieth Century

Taking up the reins in 1895 to see Barnwood House Hospital into the twentieth century was its fourth chairman, Sir Francis Adams Hyett, the son of its first chairman. He was to hold the position of Chairman of the Hospital for the exceptional time of forty-one years, with the result that its reputation as a mental Hospital grew to be one of the highest in the country.

The central block, the original house, which was used for offices and the medical superintendent's residence, either suffered a fire or was in danger of collapse, and so in 1897 was torn down and an enlarged and taller structure was built in brick.

The rebuilt Central Block.

By the turn of the century the Hospital was caring for the maximum number of patients it could satisfactorily deal with, at any one time, 160. By now the Hospital buildings extended both westward towards Church Lane, but primarily eastward towards Upton Lane.

Additional amenities for the patients such as a Theatre, a Tenpin Bowling Alley, Billiard and Snooker Rooms and an Occupational Therapy Room, all contributed to the care, treatment, and well-being of the patients.

From the photograph below, it can be seen that the extensions to the Hospital happened in stages as the need for expansion arose, because the frontages of each section are by no means uniform.

Differing roof alignments and variations in style show that this was a piecemeal development which reached its conclusion by the 1930s.

The buildings as they spread piecemeal and eastward towards Hucclecote.

Once the buildings had reached the Hospital's eastern boundary further extensions were added southward towards the gardens and brook. The addition of extensions also occurred at the western end.

At about this period, the prospects for the future of the Hospital were as good as they had been at any time throughout its history. There was a steady demand for the services it could provide, the financial position was highly satisfactory, the management was sound, there was little, if any difficulty in filling many of the positions in the Hospital, services and supplies were plentiful and therefore cheap. The future seemed assured. This continued for the next thirty to forty years during which the Hospital was either full or nearly so.

The War Years

The first interruption to the Hospital's stability was the occasion of the First World War.

As early as 1914, fourteen of the twenty-seven male staff had left for military service, rising to thirty-five men from the Hospital staff by 1917. By then, of those that had enlisted, one had been killed and eight wounded.

Six of the Hospital's attendants applied for military exemption on the grounds that they were indispensable to the Hospital.

Of the twenty-three attendants who eventually joined up, ten became Non-Commissioned officers. Perhaps reflecting the leadership qualities of a hospital attendant.

One member of the staff who served in the forces, Dr. Captain Pennant of the Royal Army Medical Corps was awarded the Distinguished Service Order for his work with the wounded. Dr Pennant was invalided out and returned to part time duties as Temporary Assistant Medical officer. This then became permanent towards the end of 1918 as part of the reorganisations following the resignation of Dr. Soutar[13].

The Hospital Committee agreed that Hospital Staff who joined the forces would be reinstated after the war, paying them the difference between military wages and what they would have earned during their absence.

The remaining staff were asked to work longer hours and have reduced leave. New, young, attendants were recruited, all of whom had to be trained.

---

[13] Dr. James Greig Soutar joined the Hospital in 1883 as Assistant Medical Officer and was later appointed Superintendent.

The Committee's report for 1916 bemoans the high turnover of male staff and the difficulty of recruiting suitable people. 'Very few are fitted either by character or capacity to be entrusted, even under supervision, with the delicate and difficult and highly responsible duties which an attendant has to discharge'. Three new recruits left soon after joining, saying "they could not stand the work".

It was also felt by the Committee that the construction of the Brockworth aerodrome and aircraft factory nearby was also influencing the availability of staff.

To encourage recruitment, male charge attendants, second attendants and night staff were given cost of living pay rises. Permission to sleep away from the Hospital was also granted. This would have been seen as a considerable benefit to male staff who were married.

Financial assistance was given by the government who awarded a war bonus of either 3, 2 or 1 shilling per week. The Hospital also paid a bonus of between £20 and £5 p.a. to remaining male attendants for loss of leave and overtime being worked.

It also became difficult to maintain an adequate supply of female nurses. Throughout the country women were being recruited to fill the vacancies left by men who were serving in the Armed Forces. The attraction of higher wages and a more congenial lifestyle away from the Hospital mean that many nurses left.
Subsequently the Nurses pay was also raised to bring this in line with other similar employments in the area and to try and stop the loss of staff.

A condition of service imposed by the Hospital was that female staff could not be employed if they were married.

A restriction that most likely resulted in many good nurses declining to work there.

The reduction in sufficient suitably trained staff eventually led to a cutback in the services the Hospital could provide, and as a result, the number of patients it could accommodate. Average numbers dropped from 154 to 135 during this period.

During 1917, the War Office was looking for places in which to nurse officers suffering from shell shock and neurasthenia. Three of the Hospital's satellite buildings - Manor House, The Wilderness and North Cottage were all offered to treat and gratuitously maintain soldiers suffering from both physical and mental exhaustion. All these offers were declined, there being sufficient accommodation elsewhere.

However, ten patients were transferred into the Hospital from asylums which had been converted into military hospitals. [14]

Separately, in 1917 the Ministry of Pensions sought places for officers from HM services who had become insane through the war conditions and who were in straitened circumstances. A maximum of £2. 2s. per week was to be paid for their accommodation. The Hospital offered 4 places provided no special treatment was needed, citing the lack of staff.

The shortage of staff applied equally to ancillary staff – both inside and outside.

On the farm three women were employed to replace the men who had left.

The purchase of an engine driven elevator to assist with harvest gathering was reported as being 'of great service', and in 1917 two soldiers worked on the farm for part of the year.

---

[14] Reflecting the building programme that occurred at the start of the war in order to create sufficient suitable hospitals for those troops that would be invalided back to Britain.

Of the gardeners, all the young men left, the remainder were assisted by three boys, and overtime being worked meant the garden remained productive and in good order. (The annual reports frequently commented that both the need for fresh flowers in the Hospital and neat and pleasant grounds were necessary for the benefit of and speedy recovery of patients.)

The Hospital managed to adhere to The Food Controller's guidelines. The initial loss of weight of some patients was halted and, in some cases, reversed by changes to their diets. The cooks coped with food rationing by using more non rationed foods. Meat was highly rationed, so the meals were supplemented with fish.

Butter was in short supply at the end 1917. The Hospital was unable to obtain their usual Irish Butter and there was no local alternative. To overcome this, more dairy cattle were purchased, and consumption of the farm's milk reduced resulting in the surplus being used to make butter, thus meeting this shortfall.

The last quarter of 1918 saw a significant change in the Senior management of the Hospital. Dr Soutar resigned for health reasons. He had been employed for 35 years and was Head Doctor for 26 years. The Matron, Miss Buckle left after 33 years, 26 as matron, due to failing health. Miss Price, Head Nurse for 15 years left to get married.

Dr Townsend was appointed successor to Soutar, and Dr Pennant was appointed to replace Dr Townsend.

Miss Edwards was appointed to replace Miss Buckle. She had been on the staff for 14 years, the last 3 as deputy to Miss Price. Miss Martin who for the previous 5 years had been a sister on the staff, replaced Miss Price.

The Hospital, having survived the difficulties of the last four years, was now adequately staffed and able to return to admitting the numbers of patients it had previously.

The newly recruited male staff were nearly all ex-army and "are intelligent and competent men". An interesting comment from the Annual Report.

Six of the male attendants who left to join up returned. Of the remainder, twelve were killed in action, and several incapacitated.

After the end of the War, there was still a difficulty in recruiting and retaining female staff. It was commented that "they were unable to settle down to steady work, doubtless due to the unrest caused by working conditions during the war".

The effect of the war on the Hospital was still being felt in 1920. Whilst the numbers of male nursing staff stayed steady, there were still many changes in senior medical staff, with many retiring and some moving to other fields. Junior female nurses still found it difficult to settle. Pay rises were awarded across most of the Hospital staff and the hours of medical staff reduced to 60 hours per week [15] (excluding meals).

The cost of living was rising, the greatest increase during 1920 was the expenditure on commodities, followed by wages and salaries. It now cost more, on average, to treat a patient than was received by them.

The Hospital committee felt they could not increase fees as many patients were on a fixed income and were being affected by increases in personal taxation.

Another impact on the Hospital was the increase in admissions of patients with long-term stress. Dr Townsend reported that this was due "to the period of strain during the long years of the war and the unrest and disquiet in peacetime" However the recovery rate was the highest ever - possibly due to the early treatment of these easily treatable disorders.

---

[15] An interesting comparison with today's working week.

Barnwood House successfully overcame the stresses and strains of the Second World War as it did those of the First.

Added to such encumbrances as the shortage of food and materials, and the compliance with numerous controls and restrictions, common to both wars was the development of aerial warfare and the threat from above.

The Hospital was fortunate to escape damage, the nearest bombs falling two hundred yards away. But a large aircraft factory in the vicinity, just a few miles eastward at Brockworth, made the area susceptible.

There was, almost nightly, the drone from raiding aircraft, the gloom of the black-out through long winter nights, the foul and penetrating fumes from the factory's protecting smoke screen and the noise of gunfire from an anti-aircraft half-battery nearby. [16]

The rigid observance of air-raid precautions and the creation of routines for the protection of patients in an emergency was an extra weight borne for an exceedingly long time. [17]

Throughout the war the Hospital posted air raid wardens on the top of the water towers at each end of the central block, as they were one of the highest points in Barnwood and offered a clear view for miles around.

---

[16] The battery was positioned in a field called '40 Acres', which is where Eastern Avenue and the TA Centre are today. It also flew one, or possibly several Barrage Balloons, much to the delight of the children of the time.

[17] These comments are almost verbatim from Tom Gale's memories of the time and expresses the frustration and tedium that must have been felt.

The Advent of the NHS

In 1905, the Royal Commission on the Poor Law and the Unemployed was set up to review the system of workhouses for assisting the poor, and to recommend changes. They advocated for institutions catering for specific groups such as children, the elderly or 'the mentally ill'. The State subsequently passed legislation requiring institutions to be provided for the care of the mentally ill who had been dependent upon their parishes for support. This relieved the Subscribers of their responsibility for this class of patient, leaving them with just their responsibility for the other two classes - the wealthy and the poor not on parochial relief. The latter were subsidised by funds derived from payments by the wealthy patients, benefactors, and legacies.

In the immediate post-war period, the future status of the Hospital and its governing body became uncertain, due to the passing by Parliament of the National Health Service Act 1946, which empowered the Minister of Health to acquire hospitals for the State. This uncertainty as to the future status of the Hospital and its governing body was eventually resolved, following W Croome, the Hospital's Chairman, along with representatives from several other registered hospitals making representation in person to the Minister. Notice was therefore received in June 1948 that the Minister had decided to "disclaim" Barnwood House from the operation of the Act. The Hospital's property and funds were thus left as they were before, in the sole possession and administration of the Governors.

The Act made provision for a free health service for all, including care in hospital when necessary. However, a part of society still depended upon, or wished for, private care to meet its needs.

The Hospital Trust, having declined the opportunity of abrogation of its responsibilities offered by the Act, continued to the best of its ability to fulfil its obligations for very nearly another quarter of a century.

Post war changes

The clarification and settlement of the future governance of the Hospital outside that of the NHS, enabled the resumption of the improvements and activities which had been interrupted by the Second World War.

Because of the early introduction of a national system of reservation of certain occupations, relatively very few of the Hospital's employees were away on military service. Nevertheless, by the end of the war some had left either to work elsewhere, for retirement or for other reasons, and the shortage became acute.

New occupations offered more attractive openings, especially for women, and this affected the recruitment for training. It soon became difficult and then impossible to find sufficient fulltime nurses, so that there had to be reliance on those employed part time.

The training school for nurses, which had for many years before the war been markedly successful, became redundant and closed.

In addition to the 'Nurses' Home' at North Cottage, conveniently situated almost opposite to the main building, a policy of providing living accommodation other than that in the Hospital, had been introduced before the war. It took the form of either building modern houses on the estate or upgrading and modernising property that the Hospital purchased. After the war, this policy was continued and extended to benefit not only nurses, but other employees whose services were essential to the efficient running of the Hospital and its estate. At one time there were over thirty houses, many of them new, occupied by staff. The rents were usually token and there was a waiting list. For many years, the provision of staff housing near at hand was a distinct advantage in obtaining and keeping employees.

The Beginning of the End

Because Barnwood was a registered hospital, there were no claims on its profits by either shareholders or investors. Consequently, all of any surplus revenue could be used to benefit the Hospital. This was done in a number of ways, such as to pay for improvements or extensions and generally adding to the amenities, or it could be set aside and invested to form a capital sum, either for some specific future use or as a general reserve.

Licensed houses and registered hospitals alike were, for many years before the Second World War, generally believed to have achieved financial results regarded as lucrative. Barnwood was no exception. In addition to the expenditure of considerable sums directly affecting the welfare of patients, it had succeeded, over the course of many years in adding to its assets by the purchases of land and, most importantly, by increasing money invested to form a substantial capital sum.

However, the unbroken pattern of years of financial success began to fade soon after the Second World War. The difficulties developed slowly but surely. The decline seems to have begun in 1947, rather insidiously and somewhat inopportunely, coinciding with the Hospital's resumption of its programme of medical research, with the resultant additional expenditure.

In only four of the remaining twenty years of the Hospital's life was the income from patients sufficient to pay for the cost of their care and treatment. Higher charges to patients could not be made to all and were within narrow limits. Sometimes they were also found to be counter-productive in that they would deter new admissions.

The Hospital's committee were also ever mindful that as a charity they had an obligation to meet, either partially or wholly, the fees of those patients who would benefit and be cured by treatment, but who could not afford it.

The Annual Reports during this time frequently comment that many of the occupants of the Hospital were elderly or incurable and had been in the Hospital for many years. As these required more intensive nursing and specialist accommodation, Dr Fleming, the Head Doctor during this time, felt that these patients were taking up resources that could be put towards helping those short-term patients who had every chance of recovery.

A policy of moving elderly patients to other hospitals to free up resources was therefore adopted. From this point onward, the number of patients admitted increased and for many of these, their stay was relatively short and so the numbers of patients resident at the end of the year remained fairly constant at about 160.

Nevertheless, the policy not to deny admission while there were beds vacant was continued even though the full fees could, more frequently, not be met.

The change, around the 1940s, to only admitting patients with a good, rather than reasonable, chance of recovery, together with newer treatments, meant that patients spent less time in the Hospital. Admissions could therefore be increased as yearly discharges almost matched yearly admissions.

During 1962 well over one half of the patients were kept for fees which were below the average cost. Inevitably the result for the year was a financial loss, and in this respect the year was a typical one of the period, with no prospect of the downward trend being reversed

From about 1960 onward, one factor that was starting to influence the number of applications for admission to the Hospital was that there were far fewer people in a position to pay for private treatment. More were taking advantage of a Health Service provided free by the state in hospitals where conditions were greatly improving and increasingly less resembling the badly over-crowded conditions of times gone by.

To counter this imbalance, many economies were made throughout the organisation, but the expenditure that could not be controlled was that of wages and salaries. Many of these were tied to those paid to those working in the National Health Service and which were increasing year by year.

These years were difficult financially, sums of varying amounts had to be found from other sources to keep the Hospital going and it was only the use of the Hospital's reserves which made survival possible.

The fact that Barnwood House was disclaimed under the National Health Service Act, 1946, and thus remained a private body under the ownership and administration of its governors, merely delayed its inevitable demise.

As late as 1962 the Committee devoted a series of meetings in an attempt to analyse the situation and to seek a remedy. The whole of the Hospital's expenditure was brought under close review and reductions were made wherever possible without lowering the standard of services to patients.

It was found that a very high proportion of expenditure for the patients was outside any control by the Committee, and that the very substantial economies which had already been made were being nullified by further wage awards and higher costs of some essential supplies at a national level.

Yet there was no serious deterioration in standards, and expenditure on work essential to maintain them was kept up.

As costs continued to rise, the gap between the amount spent on patients and that received from them grew wider. Had the number of patients been higher the extra income would have helped to narrow the gap since the overhead costs would not have increased proportionately.

Conversely, however, the costs could not be reduced in the same proportion when the number fell.

Nationally, there were never more than a dozen or so registered hospitals. Of those not acquired by the State, thus retaining their independence, only three or four of the larger ones were really in a position to carry on. This was largely because their patient numbers were high, certainly than that of Barnwood's, and so their costs could be spread, thus cushioning the effect on their reserves of assets. Additional revenue resulting from contracts to provide beds for the National Health Service also helped.

The smaller institutions including most of the licensed houses were now no longer in a position to compete and some had already closed.

While costs at Barnwood were significant, other possible causes need to be considered.

For example, the comparatively recent and impressive break-through of modern tranquillizing medicine and the concept of treatment at home reduced considerably the number of patients admitted to hospitals.

The treatment of mental and similar illnesses in the psychiatric wards of general hospitals affected the number of admissions to the private hospitals.

And finally, the social, economic, and political changes since the Second World War had been considerable and far-reaching, which inevitably contributed to the decline in private hospitals.

The situation at Barnwood could not be allowed to continue.

The Closure of the Hospital

In 1963 Dr Burrows became Head Doctor on the death of Dr Fleming.

Dr Burrows was much better qualified over financial matters than either Doctor Fleming or the Hospital's chairman, W. Croome, and he wasted no time in opening the Committee's eyes to the plight at Barnwood.

The first worry was the non-contributory pension fund. With inflation running at a high rate the capital cost of funding this scheme was in danger of overtaking the free capital. This problem was solved by handing over the scheme, plus virtually all the Hospital's investments to an Insurance Company.

In 1967, with the coffers empty and the Hospital losing money, the inevitable decision to close and sell the Hospital was taken following the conclusion that it could not be continued in its then present form.

The Committee gave themselves two years to bring this closure to a head, but then a second disaster hit. The electrical wiring throughout the entire Hospital was declared to be dangerous and despite the proposed short life of Barnwood this was put in hand at the cost of £30,000 (a very significant amount of money even then).

This job was completed some six months before the sale of the Hospital and its complete demolition[18].

The Committee believed that by taking timely action, the heavy losses associated in maintaining and staffing a large building, some of it no longer suitable for modern needs and much of it unoccupied, could be avoided.

---

[18] In mitigation of this expense, I believe the committee had no option but to immediately undertake this work for safety reasons. They were anticipating selling the Hospital as a going concern and may not have anticipated its demolition.

At the same time, it was decided to open the Manor House as a small Nursing Home. The revenue from the sale of the Hospital and grounds with a separate sale of several acres of the farmland for the construction of Walls' Ice Cream factory would provide The Committee with sufficient funds to convert the Manor House for this purpose. The smaller unit was felt to be viable and that sufficient funds to meet contingencies could be kept in reserve.

By continuing at the Manor House, a complete closure of the Hospital would be avoided, and the Hospital Trust kept alive.

As soon as the decision to close was announced, arrangements were begun for the dispersal of the Hospital's patients. Some were able to go to their own homes, with most of the others to hospitals and nursing homes elsewhere.

It took two years to close the Hospital.

There then followed the disposal of the building's furniture and contents. They were diverse and considerable. A selection was made for use at the Manor House. Some was taken, at valuation, by the St Andrews private hospital in Northampton, to which many of the patients had been transferred. The rest was to be sold by auction.

Unfortunately, a short while before opening the Manor House for patients, it suffered an arson attack which resulted in considerable damage to the furniture and fittings and some of the items destined for St Andrews were diverted to replace those lost in the fire.

Bruton Knowles held an auction in the Hospital in order to dispose of much that was left.

The auction took place on the five days Monday 17th to Friday 21st of June 1968.

Amongst the lots for sale were antiques, Persian rugs, beds, wardrobes, dressers, chests, carpets, curtains, dining tables, chairs, bookcases, linen, and domestic china. A Rathbone dentist's chair was amongst the lots. The garden machinery and implements were also sold off. There were two baby's baths. In all, some 2,100 lots were on offer.

The tablecloths from No2. Ladies Dining room were purchased by Barnwood's Ladies Circle and used for many years as tablecloths and napkins in the Parish Reading Room.

The auction realised some £10K and is still talked about by those and their families who attended. Tales are told of the incredible bargains that were to be had. For example, Turkish rugs and carpets were sold for between £50 and £90.

£80 was paid for a Dennis fire-fighting trailer pump on pneumatic tyres. This pump was the first appliance the Hospital's fire crew owned and would be manhandled to the scene of the fire. Later on, the Hospital also owned a fire engine to which this trailer would be attached.
What happened to this engine has yet to be established.

The Hospital is Sold.

The prospectus for the sale of the Hospital was issued in 1968.

It described in detail the Hospital's buildings, gardens, and grounds that were for sale, comprising of some 14 ½ acres.

The sale was to be by private treaty.

The cover of the Sales Brochure.
This is believed to be the only coloured picture of the Hospital

At first the Committee were looking to sell the Hospital and its grounds to a purchaser who would use them for a similar purpose as the Trust had. The Sales Prospectus detailed the layout of the Hospital with the obvious intention that it should be sold as a fully functioning Private Hospital.

The offering did not include the Trust's land to the south of the Wotton Brook, nor the farmland and buildings to the north of Barnwood Road

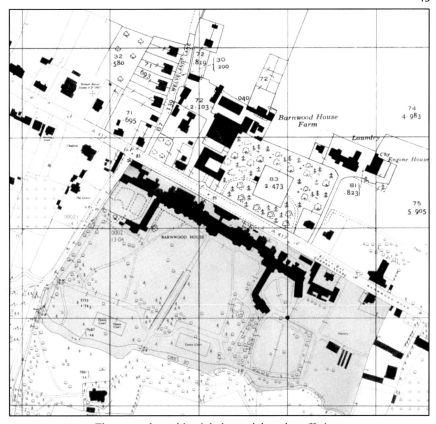

The area coloured in pink denoted the sales offering.

The Wotton Brook; the boundary wall to Manor House lands; Barnwood Road; and Church Lane determined its boundary.

The Market Garden, of about 2½ acres, had 7 heated greenhouses, 7 sets of cold frames, 2 temporary greenhouses and a potting shed.
However, this offering of a fully functioning hospital and grounds did not find a buyer.
The fact that the Hospital was closing for financial reasons and that Gloucester City Council were considering making a Tree Preservation Order on the land, possibly deterred potential purchasers.

50

On the 28th of March 1969, Bruton Knowles, on behalf of the Hospital Trustees, submitted a proposal to the Local Planning Authority for the demolition of the Hospital buildings and for residential houses to be built on that land. The consent for this was granted on July 4th.

This enabled the Trustees to place the building and now, a larger area of grounds, for sale by auction.

The auction took place at the Gloucester Guildhall on Tuesday 30th of September 1969.

Offered for sale now was 19 acres, of which 7 acres had outline planning permission for residential development. This permission specified that the developers should build high quality housing, preferably at a density of six units to the acre.

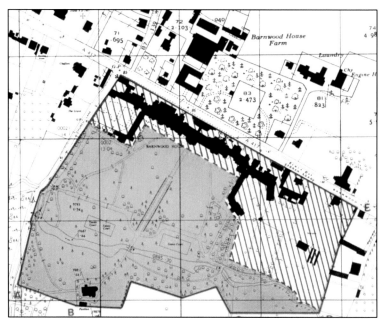

The second offering.

The land to the south, including some land across the Wotton Brook up to the Chapel and adjacent cricket pavilion was also part of the sale offering. On the plan above, the hatched area is designated for housing whilst outlined in red, but not hatched, is the area that will become the Barnwood Arboretum (north of the Brook), and Barnwood Park, (to the south the brook.).

Two houses 154 and 156 Barnwood Road, to the east of the building were also offered for sale.

The Conveyance, dated 3rd of December 1969, covering the sale, identifies five parties involved in the disposition of the land. The apportionment was made 'in order to carry out the most beneficial form of development of the land, to protect the amenities of the area and to perfect (satisfy) the wishes of all the interested parties'.

There were a number of 'interested parties': -

Firstly, were the vendors, The Trustees of The Barnwood House Hospital Charity, Captain Peter Gibbs, Lord Banbury, and their solicitor Robert Hutton. They sold the property for £75,000, a sum which was in excess of the reserve placed on it by the Charity Commissioners.

Secondly, the builder William Gavaghan of 19, Clarence Street Gloucester (Gavaghan Ltd). He paid the Trustees £20,000 for the land that today is known as Grovelands.

Thirdly, Moorgarth Developments from London, who would construct the Housing which is today known as Cherston Court. They paid the Trustees £48,000 for this portion of land and the land across the brook.

Fourthly, local solicitor, Robert (Robin) Morris who purchased the main house and its gardens to the south for £7,000. He paid this directly to the Trustees, thereby making up the remainder of the sale fee.

Lastly were 'The Mayor, Alderman and Citizens of Gloucester' (The Corporation).

One of the planning requirements was that the purchasers would donate the land on the south side of the brook, together with the Chapel which stood on it, to the Local Authority as a public park.

Robert Morris, Gavaghan and Moorgarth therefore conveyed this part of their land, that to the south of the brook, to the Corporation 'for the benefit and protection of the adjoining and neighbouring land….'

This parcel of land eventually became Barnwood Park.

This conveyance was a significant and altruistic action for it ensured that the heart of Barnwood would remain free of development and become a place of peace and reflection.

The conveyance detailed several agreements and specified numerous restrictions and covenants which were placed on the parties involved in this sale. Worthy of mention are the following: -

Robert Morris was given access into Grovelands from his land. This was at the end of the cul-de-sac. He also had right of access over the brook into the Council's land in order to maintain and repair the footbridge. He had to put a gate on the southern end of this bridge.

Moorgarth were to build a bridge connecting the Council's land to the south of the brook with the new Cherston Court estate. This was to allow the council access. They were also to clean the Wotton Brook and undertake some minor works at the weir by Church Lane within six months of the conveyance.

The council were required to ensure that the park was kept for the enjoyment of the public, to maintain and repair the sides of the brook and weir, not to erect any dwelling house or building on the land apart from a summerhouse, shelter or similar ornamental erection suited to park land provided for the public, and to keep the area in good repair and well stocked with shrubs and trees.

The Chapel on the parkland could only be used for such purposes that were not inconsistent with the use as a public parkland.

So, by the end of 1969 the Trustees had sold the Hospital building and nineteen acres of land. The proceeds were then invested.

Now all The Hospital Trust owned in Barnwood, was the Manor House in its five-and-a-half acres, a number of houses, the bulk of the land north of Barnwood Road which was still being farmed, and land south of the chapel up to the boundary with Coney Hill Hospital, today Abbeymead Avenue.

Soon after the 1969 sale, the two wings of the Hospital building were demolished, leaving just the central block.

The demolition was carried out by Gavaghan Ltd.

So, what was to become of the house that Robin Morris purchased?

The House Becomes a Home

In February 1970, Robin Morris obtained planning permission to convert this house into a domestic dwelling and to close the vehicular access onto Barnwood Road, replacing it with one through the newly constructed housing estate of Grovelands and with a pedestrian gate in the Barnwood Road wall. This gate was certainly there by 1978/79 though today, evidence of this is fragmentary.

Robin and his family are recorded in the 1971 Electoral Roll as living there, so it can be assumed that they took occupation either late 1970 or early 1971.

For most of its existence the Hospital had an underground service tunnel running the whole length of the building. This was long, wide, tall, and in many places tiled.

In conversation with Robin, he recalled how his children used to ride their bikes up and down this tunnel under their house.

This tunnel still runs under the gardens of some of the houses in both Cherston Court and Grovelands.

A resident of Cherston Court commented to me that the tunnel was never filled in, and when a garage was being built in Cherston Court, the ground opened up, and a worker fell through to a toilet below.

Another time a digger fell into the tunnel and almost disappeared.

The following pictures, taken by Robin Morris, show the grounds and building soon after his purchase.

As there are no houses either side, and the garage to the east of the house has not yet been built, this photograph would have been taken about 1970, soon after the sale.

The tower of the Hospital's Coach House can be seen in the distance at the left of this picture.

The house from the southeast.

The picture above shows the corner of one of the Hospital's tennis courts, and between that and the house can be seen the line of a wall that may have been part of the Hospital's gardens.

The new developments of Cherston Court, seen on the left, and that of Grovelands on the right, are now established.

The house as seen from the Barnwood Road frontage.

The view of the wall and Barnwood road from the building's main entrance.

Although, today, this area is now well established as an arboretum, it is still possible to see some remains of the hospital's summerhouse, paths and supporting walls.

Robin Morris decided to sell and move away from Gloucester and so the property was put up for auction on Friday 7th of March 1975, at the Plough Hotel Cheltenham. The auctioneers were Harrods of Cheltenham.

Ada Rosina Bassett ran 'The Flame School of Dance and Drama' which was then in London Road. She and her husband, The Baron von Kuhne, had been looking for a property in which they could run her dance school

The solicitor who was advising them was Robin Morris who suggested the house that he was currently selling might be suitable. Although they were advised that the property had restrictions, they felt that these could be overcome. They purchased the House and moved in.

In her autobiography, 'Just me' she said, "But it did not work out as the restrictions could not be removed, therefore it was useless for our purpose. Also, the estate houses on either side were swarming with children on bicycles".

They therefore decided to sell up and move to Stroud.

And so, the property again came on the market, and early in 1977 Barnwood House was occupied, this time by Mr and Mrs Forrest and their two children.

It would seem that the Forrests had plans for the house for they applied to have the second floor turned into 3 'Bed Sitters'.

permission was granted in April 1977.

About 1978, Mrs Forrest ran part of her home as an overflow boarding house for Selwyn School in Matson on the outskirts of Gloucester. Primarily for weekly boarders, though some pupils stayed there throughout the term.

It might also have been used for both occasional and short-term boarding pupils. It is thought that her daughter was a pupil at Selwyn which was why Mrs Forrest offered to take the overflow.

They were granted permission for the erection of an external fire escape in March 1979. Probably as a requirement for running the boarding house. Later, 21st September 1979, a covenant restricting the use of the land was obtained by some of the residents of houses who bordered the land owned by the Forrests. This may have been to ensure any future plans Mr and Mrs Forrest had would not have an impact on them.

It remained a Selwyn School boarding house until about 1984 when this function ceased, and pupils were no longer boarded at Barnwood. Mrs Forrest then let out her rooms.

Many of the boarders had fond memories of staying there and these are some of the comments that have been posted on social media.

"Mrs Forrest was the matron and mainly managed Barnwood House alone as Mr Forrest was often away. My sister and I boarded there from about 1978 to about 1984, when we were moved back to Taylor House. I have very fond memories of boarding at Barnwood House".

"On the first floor there were two dorms at the back, with a bathroom between the two. There were about 5-6 girls in each dorm, with 2 or 3 sets of bunk beds. Then at the front of the house, to the right of the stairs there was the senior's dorm. It was a lovely big bright room, with about 6 single beds. The big room opposite the senior's dorm was used as a common room for watching TV and doing homework."

"The hallway at the top of the stairs was really wide, and there was a dining table against the right wall. Between the hallway and the senior's dorm was a kitchenette area and the dumb waiter where all the cooked food from the main kitchen downstairs was transported up to us boarders." The kitchen was on the ground floor, to the left of the main entrance.

"The owners living room was to the right of the front door". (*This was at the rear of the house overlooking the gardens*)

"A shower room was immediately to the right, and their daughter's room to the left. Directly opposite was the Tuck Shop".

"I guess there were other bedrooms at the back, but I never saw them, they were private."

"Mrs Forrest always rented out the upper floor to lodgers, while boarders occupied the middle floor. They were forbidden to go up the stairs, which were directly opposite the main stairs, to this level."

It seems that the family and boarders occupied the ground and first floors whilst other residents occupied the second floor and possibly the attic.

The family kept livestock which included sheep, rabbits, a goat, geese, ducks (boarders collected the duck eggs), and a donkey, which boarders used to ride, and sometimes scary bullocks which used to chase them round the field.

With the demise of the Selwyn School arrangement, Mr and Mrs Forrest needed to maximise their use of this building. Firstly, In July 1983, planning permission was obtained for the house to be converted into a 'Elderly Persons Home' for 12 residents. This did not come to fruition. Later, in December 1986 outline planning permission was granted for the erection of 5 detached houses and garages. Again, a venture that did not happen. In November 1987 permission was granted for the house to be used as a Nursing Home. Again, plans were thwarted, for in December of that year permission was refused for the construction of a two-story extension to give an additional bedroom and living accommodation to the Nursing Home. The Forrests therefore reverted back to letting out their rooms and the property was set out as a number of self-contained bedsit units. The following May (1988) permission was granted to convert the third floor into a self-contained flat.

In June 1990, Mrs Forrest applied for outline planning permission for 6 detached houses and an estate road on the House land. Not surprisingly, this was refused. Having seemingly exhausted all her options, she decided to sell the house and grounds, but was unable to find a buyer.

This picture shows the house and somewhat unkempt grounds, believed to be at the time of its occupation by the Forrest family. Sheep can be seen in grounds. The fencing intended to stop them falling into the water is damaged and the grass appears to be heavily trodden. The bridge has gone just leaving the north pair of pillars.

The Final Demolition

The demolition of the house. The picture is taken from Pegasus Court.

The fate of this remnant of Barnwood House Hospital was undecided for several years. Maintaining it might have been beyond the resources of the Forrests.

It attracted the interests of several organisations and developers and was considered by them for many uses. A film Company wished to buy it, the charity Emmaus were interested in using it for accommodation, and one developer wished to convert it into high quality apartments.

Sometime around 1995 the house and grounds were sold to the developer Paul Hubbard. By then the house was in a dilapidated state.
Negotiations between all parties involved took some years, consent being given once it was agreed that the gardens would be sold to the Council for use as an arboretum.

On the 14ᵗʰ June 2000 Captiva Builders put in a planning request for the demolition of the house, the erection of 6 houses, and the provision of a public open space.

This was granted on the 25ᵗʰ April 2001. Even then there were 15 conditions imposed which needed addressing before development could take place.

Captiva Properties of Cheltenham developed the site. Beechgrove of Cheltenham demolished the House and constructed the six houses. The Architects were ASTAMS of Gloucester.

The demolition of the building was by a specialist company hired by Beechgrove. They recycled much of the building, most notably the three fireplaces, one on each floor, which were of very high quality.

This is a picture of one of these, taken by Robin Morris when he lived there. The fireplaces were said to be 6ft by 5 ft.

Apparently, these were boarded up later and only discovered when the building was being demolished.

On the 25ᵗʰ April 2001, Captiva sold to Gloucester City Council the land to the south of the House up to the brook for the sum of £1. This area was then developed as the Arboretum.

And so, the 'Gentleman's Residence' of 1856 which became a hospital of significance, finally disappeared from the skyline of Barnwood.

Continuation at The Manor House

When the decisions to close the main Hospital were being made, there was a desire to continue, albeit in a much-reduced form. The creation of a nursing home for a small number of patients at the Manor House was deemed to be a way to achieve this.

Since 1939, the building had been used as a Nurses' Home, but was now not needed for this purpose.

The rear of the building circa. 1950 when it was a Nursing Home.

One of the conditions for this new self-supporting and self-contained unit was that it should be financially viable. The minimum number of patients to make it so was twenty, and the alterations and improvements, including a conversion of separate rooms into a dormitory were made on this basis.

The building was refurbished, a small rear extension was added, and a lift installed. The very old tiles were removed from the north slope of the roof and replaced with asbestos slates to match the rest of the roof. The entrance from the roadway was improved and the orchard behind the Manor House cleared of undergrowth.

Shortly before the refurbished Manor House opened, the building suffered an arson attack when a serious fire broke out on the night of the 16/17th of March 1968 which led to a delayed opening.

Eventually nineteen of the remaining Hospital patients were transferred there and it opened in May 1968.

What remained of the Hospital's administration operated out of Manor House and would do so for many years to come.

In 1970 a small extension was added to the rear as a day room for the patients.

In the first year it was found that twenty-three beds were the maximum and the actual average occupied was twenty-one. Having been transferred from the Hospital, its patients were very confused, many of them also frail and elderly.

The care in the Manor attained much the same high standard as that of Barnwood House, despite some obvious handicaps such as the inherent differences in physical space and environment.

As a nursing home, it was intended to be financially independent, capable of supporting patients to the same high standards of Barnwood House. Envisaged as a self-supporting project and expected to be viable financially with 20 patients, against a bed capacity of 23.

Even though patients' fees set at the time were relatively modest, as many as fourteen long term patients of insufficient means were subsidised by the Trustees from their limited sources of income.

Apart from during the first few years, rising costs meant that regular subsidies were required. As early as 1973, the costs of running the Nursing Home had increased to the point where it became necessary to raise fees for those patients who were not subsidised. The new standard weekly fees from 1st July 1974 became £26.25 for shared accommodation and £31.50 for a single room.

From 1974 onwards the country suffered a period of rampant inflation which reached a peak of almost 20% in 1975. The effect of this, coupled with three huge national pay awards for nurses in 1974 and 1975, two of them to be back dated, caused the Nursing Home operating costs to spiral out of control.

With costs rising at an unprecedented rate, subsidies became necessary to such an extent that the Trustees had doubts as to whether these could be justified when concentrated to the benefit of so few.

At the same time, new legislation requiring more floor space for each bed meant that bed capacity had to be cut from 23 to 20, so reducing, still further, income from fees.

In economic terms, the double effect of this squeeze - soaring costs on the one hand and restricted income from fees on the other - meant that much of the Trustees' limited resources were now being used to maintain just 20 patients.

Worthwhile savings in the costs of operating the Nursing Home were not feasible without a big drop in nursing standards for by then, salaries and wages accounted for about 80% of total costs. Attempts to increase fees for those patients who were not subsidised met with only limited success due to the difficult economic climate and to increasing competition from the National Health Service. It was now recognised that with the expansion of the NHS, health care needs had changed dramatically and that, as a consequence, survival was becoming more and more difficult for small independent very specialised nursing services such as the Manor House Nursing Home provided.

Against this difficult background, with the greatest reluctance, the Trustees decided that the Nursing Home would have to be closed if the future of the Trust as an independent charity was to be safeguarded for the benefit of future generations.

The Trustees realised that, in taking this decision, they were severing their last direct link with nursing care after a period of 150 years, but they saw no alternative.

The closure was planned for the 31st July 1977 and six months' notice of the intention was given to all the Nursing Home staff and to those responsible for patients' affairs.

All possible help was then given to assist relatives and friends in placing patients in hospitals or nursing homes appropriate to their needs. For those patients of insufficient means, the Trustees undertook to assist them financially for up to five years.

True to the highest traditions of their profession, the nursing staff maintained the morale of patients during this difficult run-down period so that when the closure occurred, it was achieved with some dignity for patients and staff.

The Manor Day Care Centre

The physical limitations of the Manor House as a Nursing Home had been fully recognised by the Trustees, but it was felt that, in later years, when additional money became available from the lease or sale of some of the Trust's 200 acres of freehold land, it should be possible to build a modern purpose-built nursing home in the grounds of the Manor House and to use the Manor House for other purposes. It was also considered desirable to build and operate Sheltered Housing in tandem with the new Nursing Home to meet what was seen as a rapidly growing need in the community.

In preparation for such a possibility, the Trustees obtained the agreement of the Charity Commissioners in 1975 to widen the Trust's objects, [19] making it possible for the Trust to help not only the mentally ill and the mentally handicapped as they had done, but also the physically handicapped and the aged and infirm. In addition, the Trustees were empowered to build and run sheltered housing and to use any surplus funds to assist other charities with objects similar to their own or to help individuals who qualified for such help.

This was a significant change and had far reaching effects enabling the Trust to continue into the 21st Century.

Once the decision had been taken to close the Nursing Home, the Trustees straightaway considered how best to pursue their new objectives.

Research had shown there was a big gap in the Local Authority's provision of day care for the very many lonely, elderly, and disabled people in the community.

Consequently, it was decided as a first step to set up a Day Care Centre in the Manor House.

_____

[19] The objects are the beneficiaries of a trust

The intention was to provide a subsidised 'home from home' for about 30 or so guests daily, Monday to Friday, giving them companionship and their families and carers some respite.

After some re-equipping and refurbishment, extensive publicity, and the holding of a number of 'Open Days', the Manor Day Home was opened on the 1st of December 1977.

The facilities on offer to day guests for just £2 a day included the provision of transport to and from their homes, morning coffee, a proper lunch and afternoon tea, as well as the opportunity to meet other people in a 'homely' atmosphere and to pursue hobbies and interests - was exceptional value, especially for pensioners.

Even so, the Trustees recognised they were breaking new ground and that it would take some time for such a venture to become widely known, accepted, and fully utilised, especially in view of the widespread reputation of the Hospital as a mental institution in Barnwood for almost 150 years.

Although the momentum of advertising was maintained after the opening, attendance was disappointingly low for the whole of the first year and numbers did not start to pick up very much until the spring of 1979.

After that, the Day Home's popularity increased - mainly through word of mouth - to the point where, by the autumn of 1979, the demand for places was greater than the Home's capacity. Numbers then had to be restricted to about 30 a day and a waiting list was opened.

The Trustees were encouraged to see the Day Home being fully utilised, but they recognised that this greater activity would result in higher operating costs and a widening gap between those costs and the income from guests which, at the end of 1979, two years after it opened, was still £2 a day.

Whilst the running of the Day Home was subsidised, which was considered to be a proper use of charitable funds since the benefit was being widely spread over some hundreds of day guests, the Trustees decided to review fees annually and to increase them modestly in order to keep the subsidy within reasonable bounds.

The Manor House as a Day Care Centre.

The space and facilities at the Manor House were now seen as inadequate to meet the growing needs of the Day Home and in 1981, a rear single storey annexe was constructed to provide an additional day room a hairdressing salon, a small store, and modern facilities. The kitchen and service rooms at the eastern end were extended, and completely modernised, with further facilities being added on both floors.

At the same time, the use of more and better transport, as well as a few more staff, meant that about 45 guests a day could now be taken without upsetting the 'homely' atmosphere.

The range of facilities available to guests was by now quite wide and included hairdressing, assisted baths for the disabled, talks and entertainments, various arts and crafts and outings. Practical help and counselling were also available.

The Trust also provided accommodation from March 1978 for a chiropody clinic run by the Area Health Authority as a free local service for the elderly and infirm.

Not only were these facilities greatly appreciated by the guests, but for many of them, the social interaction that they had when visiting the Centre was of inestimable benefit.

Over the years the Manor Day Home continued to provide a much-valued service to the community and the Trustees were proud of the high reputation it enjoyed not only in Gloucester but in Cheltenham, Stroud, and the surrounding areas.

Sheltered Housing

Soon after the establishment of the Day Care Centre, the Trustees began to consider building and operating sheltered housing for elderly and handicapped people in the grounds of the Manor House.

At the time it was generally accepted that although sheltered housing was in its infancy in future years it would become needed on an ever-increasing scale to meet the demands of a growing population of older people.[20]

For some time, the Trustees had been active behind the scenes in looking in some depth at existing schemes and considering how a suitable project might fit into their future plans.

The initial intention was to run such a scheme quite separately from the then existing Manor Nursing Home yet having links with it. The eventual closure of the Nursing Home and the creation of the Day Care Centre did nothing to change these ambitions.

The original intention was to pay for the development of the housing by selling the leasehold interest in the bungalows. However, the effect of far-reaching leasehold reforms under way in 1980 meant that lessees or even tenants might possibly acquire the right to buy the freehold of the property they occupied.

Because the bungalows were to be built on Trust land, this effectively ruled out the possibility of selling leases or even creating tenancies, and the only basis on which a Scheme could go forward was by the creation of 'Licences' which gave occupants no entitlement to acquire the freehold.

The effect of this change was to delay the Trustees' involvement until they had sufficient funds of their own to build a first phase of bungalows.

---

[20] The following has been taken from the Gale/Church histories with some editing.

Eventually in December 1980 Glevum Estates, a reputable local firm of speculative builders, were appointed to design in close consultation with the Trustees, and build a first phase of 18 bungalows, each centrally heated and well insulated with two bedrooms and a patio garden.

The work was expected to take about nine months to complete at a fixed price of £344,000 to be paid for by the sale of investments.

It involved first the demolition of the Victorian stables and outbuildings to the west of the Manor House (used as workshops and storerooms), as well as a derelict cottage known as 160 Barnwood Road.

Prior to the building work, the grounds of the Manor House had consisted of two large lawned areas near the house with a sizeable orchard below that across the whole width of the site sloping down to the Wotton Brook. The site was quickly cleared, and construction proceeded apace. The first six bungalows, including the Warden's, were completed, and handed over in June 1981. The remaining 12 were handed over progressively until completion of the whole phase in October 1981. Landscaping of the disturbed areas began as soon as building work finished and in the following Spring, a garden was created around the new development, designed by a landscape architect working closely with the Trustees. These grounds provided a pleasant environment for the residents.

Meanwhile, the Scheme had been advertised to attract a Warden and its first residents.

The Trust took the greatest care w in choosing a Warden with a proven background of 'grass roots' community work, because this was seen as a key appointment which could determine the success or failure of the Trustees' first venture into Sheltered Housing.

Mrs. Flora Rowley was chosen as the Warden with her husband Reg in eager voluntary support.

The first phase buildings.

One of the first residents acted as relief warden to ensure that Mr & Mrs Rowley had a little free time to themselves and that a warden was available to residents for 24 hours a day every day of the year.

The advertising was expected to generate a flood of applicants for residence in the scheme and so it proved to be.

For each applicant a process of interview and research was undertaken to assess their social needs and to prove their eligibility on medical grounds. Generally speaking, those in the greatest need were given priority although it had first to be established by the Trustees' medical advisor that applicants were perfectly capable of living alone with just the background support of a warden and nothing more, except possibly for those community services already available to them - a home help or a district nurse.

In other words, those likely to need full-time care or nursing in the foreseeable future would for their own sake not be considered, to avoid the trauma of an early move on to a residential home or a nursing home.

The Trustees were at pains to show that the process of selection of residents was not only fair and just but that it was seen to be so.

A balance of ages and capabilities was aimed at with 'good neighbourliness' in support of the warden a central theme.

The Warden and her husband quickly made their presence felt and showed themselves to be wonderfully caring people for whom nothing was too much trouble. They created a feeling of true companionship within the community and went to endless trouble in organising social events for the residents. They made themselves freely available to residents, regardless of the day or time of day.

Some residents attended the Day Home as guests and the less ambulant had lunches provided by the Day Home delivered to them on trays, sometimes by the Warden, sometimes by Day Home staff.
In addition, the kitchen, lounge, and dining room in the Day Home were made available to the warden on a number of weekends for social events organised for the residents.

The attractive grounds of the Manor House were available to both residents and Day Home guests giving them further opportunities to meet socially.

It was the Trustees' intention to build a second phase of Sheltered Housing at a later date when funds were available after first gaining experience in running Sheltered Housing. They spent some time determining how best the newly created Sheltered Housing and the Day Home communities could work together to mutual advantage.
This breathing space proved especially valuable.
The time was also used to look critically at the design of the existing bungalows by inviting the warden and the residents to comment on the layout so that their experience could be borne in mind at the design stage of the second generation of sheltered homes.

As the first Scheme had proved such a success, Eric Cole & Partners were appointed in 1984 to design a second phase of bungalows. They offered the choice of two different designs within a budget figure of half a million pounds.

The first Scheme was for an open plan layout similar to that of the existing phase and the other was for a more integrated scheme with bungalows grouped in squares of four facing inwards, under a 'pagoda' canopy and linked by covered ways. The Trustees preferred the closer-linked scheme for which detailed planning approval was granted in April 1985.

The new scheme consisted of 22, one-bedroomed bungalows, built in groups of four, with each opening into a central corridor. These single bedroom units offered a greater level of security and comfort for residents.

A two-bedroomed warden's bungalow (for a Deputy Warden to assist in running the enlarged Scheme), an office for the Wardens, a common room large enough for social gatherings of 40 people, two overnight 'guest rooms' and a specially equipped bathroom were included in the design.

Barnwood Builders were awarded the Contract in October 1985 and commenced on site the following month.

The Scheme was completed and handed over in September 1986.

There was now a need to maintain a "clearway" for traffic past the front of the Manor House to and from this new phase. Combined with the increased use of the Day Home it meant that the existing space for car parking was quite insufficient for everyday use.

The Trustees therefore decided to convert ''the lower lawn'' (at the north-eastern corner of the grounds) into a small car park providing 23 extra spaces, as well as a block of four garages for the use of the new sheltered housing residents. Work on this small project was completed in 1989.

When planning approval was given for the car park, and to surrounding it with landscaping and planting to soften the effect, approval was also given on grounds of public safety, to fell two mature Austrian pines which overhung the edge of the proposed car park. These trees, in the north-eastern part of the site, had given cause for concern for many years.

There were originally fourteen very tall Austrian Pines (Pinus Nigra) - all of them protected - in this north-eastern corner of the site just inside the boundary wall. Six of them faced Barnwood Road and eight adjoined Upton Lane. Two of those which faced Upton Lane were blown down during severe gales - one in 1984 and one in 1986.

The first, in the early hours of 8th February 1984, fell across the boundary wall into Upton Lane. It demolished a section of the wall, completely blocked Upton Lane to traffic and finished up in the garden of No 1 Upton Lane, narrowly missing the house and demolishing part of its boundary fence. Local Authority workmen armed with a mobile crane and various chain saws, were quickly on the scene but it was not until mid-afternoon that day that the giant tree carcass and all the resultant debris had been removed and the road re-opened to traffic. The Trustees' maintenance staff assisted the owners of the house in restoring their garden to something like normality.

The second tree came down during a storm on the 24th March 1986 when a passing cyclist was injured and treated in hospital for concussion, shock and cuts. Without doubt, the result would have been far more serious had he taken the full impact. Unfortunately, the garden of No 1 Upton Lane again suffered damage and traffic flow in Upton Lane was disrupted for a second time.

After the first of these incidents, the Trustees expressed their extreme concern to the Local Authority on the grounds of public safety and sought special permission to remove all of these tall pines, some of which were more than 100 feet high, notwithstanding the Tree Preservation Order on them.

These requests were consistently refused on the grounds that the trees were fit and healthy and that it was the freak storm conditions that had caused the two trees to be uprooted.

However, as part of the roadwork improvements in connection with the Abbeymead Housing development, nine of these trees were demolished to permit the boundary wall to be repositioned.

In all then, 11 of the 14 Austrian pines had been removed, 9 deliberately and 2 accidentally. The three remaining specimens are along the wall near the garden/maintenance workshop. The trees lost were replaced by young pines - Pinus Maritima - a variety approved by the Local Authority.

The map below shows the house and its grounds at this time.

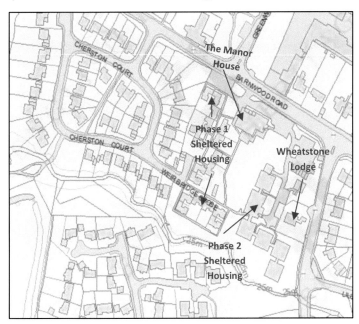

A Caring and Innovative Hospital

The management of the Hospital always considered that it was important to have as many suitable amenities for as many patients as could benefit from them.

Some of these amenities were introduced at the very beginning and over the following years they were added to as the need arose.

Great efforts were made to ensure that the patients had both entertainment and suitable leisure. For the men there was a skittle alley, billiards and snooker and the male members of staff were encouraged to participate with the patients in playing these games.

The Skittle Alley and to the left, the Billiard Room.

This is another picture of the Billiard Room, which was off the Skittle Alley. Both of these were built about 1887 when the ground floor of the western (male) wing was extended with additional bedrooms. About 1946 this area was converted into research laboratories.

Another Billiard Room was in a large day room in the west wing, overlooking the gardens. Most likely refurbished when the skittle alley and second billiard room were replaced by the research laboratories

.

The value of entertainment was also recognised, and an entertainment hall was built early on in the Hospital's life with a wide stage, allowing for numerous regular concerts, events, and lectures. Later on, it became an attractive dance hall, whose teak-lined floor, was said to be one of the best dance floors in the area.

From 1931, every Thursday afternoon and evening a film was shown. This was punctuated with music from a piano as the reels were changed on the single projector. These were very popular as the Hospital showed many of the top films of the time as they did their rounds of Gloucester's cinemas. By 1935 a sound system for this had been installed. The records do not tell if a second projector had been purchased to go with this. Ground floor plans identify a small 'cinema box' room outside the Hall opposite the stage, so one could assume that this had become a reasonably sophisticated activity.

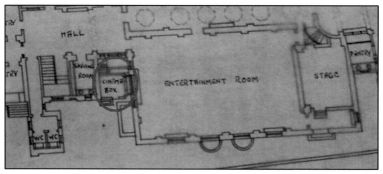

The cinema box at the end of the entertainment room.

Before the advent of television, amateur dramatics were popular, and one can imagine many a hopeful thespian treading these boards hoping for stardom.

Local choirs frequently visited to entertain both staff and patients.

The Hall.

Whenever there was a dance in the hall, for some reason, the band or the orchestra would be installed on the stage secreted behind tall flowers and vegetation. It would be heard rather than seen.

Attendance was not restricted to Hospital staff and patients, for many a local Barnwood dignitary was invited to attend. Those who attended often recalled the grandeur of the occasion.

Once a year, a special dance was given as a reward to the staff for all their hard work. Traditionally the first dance was led by the Medical Superintendent and the Matron.

Staff were very aware of the strict hierarchy of the Hospital and that they were expected to maintain their station both in their work and in their social relationships. One story is told of a member of staff who, when it was discovered that he intended taking to a dance his lady friend who was "only" a parlour maid, was firmly told that this was inappropriate and that they were not to attend.

From May till September there were cricket matches each Saturday, and although help had to be relied upon from the outside in the form of one or two stock batsmen and bowlers, who received a small payment for their services, the bulk of the team consisted of patients and staff. The opponents were local teams chosen for their suitably moderate prowess and an understanding, developed in the course of matches played, of some harmless peculiarities which might be encountered in unusual opponents. An example of these, a triviality, was the insistence of one patient, a splendidly accurate bowler, in directing a bemused fielder to move first one way, then the other and finally "on that daisy". Still in character the same player kept up a running commentary forecasting which particular ball of the over would dismiss the batsman and orally attempting to needle him, but in a refined way.

Not only was the cricket enjoyed by the players and the handful of supporters brought in by the visiting team but also by the lady patients sitting in the cricket pavilion. There, with a grandstand view, they were at a safe distance from the occasional six and in a position to view and enjoy, if not always the actual game, then a traditional English summer scene.

A view from the cricket pitch with the cricket pavilion on the left, the chapel in the centre and a sight screen on the right.

As early as 1930 an occupational therapy officer had been appointed so that classes in various handicrafts such as weaving, and basket-making could be conducted with expert tuition.

Later a purpose-built room was constructed at the end of an extension that led out into the eastern part of the gardens and a separate department was formed. This large room, overlooking the gardens, had a beautiful, curved ceiling which took ten gallons of paint to cover. It also had its walls covered in flock paper.

The activities were extended to include physical exercises and Morris dancing. As well as tuition to the patients, instruction was given in various crafts to the nurses so that teaching could be carried on by them in various rooms around the Hospital.

Classes in ballroom dancing with a live orchestra were begun in 1937.

The Occupational Therapy Room.

An amenity much appreciated by those who were able to travel were the annual visits to the seaside where, for many years, a house was taken for the months of May and June in such places as Scarborough, Tenby, or Torquay. Parties of patients would be taken there for several week at a time accompanied by their nurses and attendants, and often in the company of the superintendent and his wife. The extra cost involved was shared according to ability to pay and over the years many patients with limited means had a month's holiday away for payments well below the actual cost and in some instances free.

For therapeutic reasons, patients were driven into the countryside, another diversion greatly valued by them. Early on, transport was by horse-drawn carriage, conveniently housed in the stables and coach-house which had been built on the other side of the road.

The horses and carriage outside the Coach House, c1910.

It is said that each patient would be seated between two attendants and the patient's legs covered with a blanket on which the attendants would sit. This not only gave the patient warmth and comfort but also ensured they could not leap from the carriage and escape.

The charges for these trips varied according to the patients' financial means, and as some charges were merely nominal or waved completely, the benefits were extended to a large number of patients.

The carriage and horses were retired and a motor car for use by the Hospital was bought in 1920 with another a little later. With these two cars, the daily routine, which lasted for many years, was a country drive and shopping in the morning, and usually two country drives in the afternoon.

Over time, the Coach House housed cars, vans, and the Hospital fire engine.
The building has changed little over the years.

A recent picture of the Coach House.

A religious service was held twice weekly in the chapel in the grounds, and often as many as one-half of the patients resident at a time were able to attend.

The chapel was in regular use; all attendants and servants who could sing were expected to attend to form the choir.

The Hospital had its own chaplain. The first was Minor Canon Haines, who on his death was succeeded by the Reverend Christopher Naylor, headmaster of the Crypt School.

Naylor was the non-residentiary chaplain to the Hospital for 38 years from about 1872 until his untimely death in 1910 whilst riding his tricycle in Cheltenham. He was in his 76th year.

He was replaced by the Reverend Edward Roberts, and in 1951 Mervyn Hughes, vicar of Hucclecote, was appointed Chaplain. He remained its chaplain till at least 1966.

The appointment in 1958 of the Reverend Michael Seacome as vicar of Barnwood bought a strong musical tradition to St Lawrence, and often the choir with their organist would sing for services in the Chapel, whilst they were led by the Hucclecote vicar as Chaplain.

Inside the chapel.

The Prospectus

The Hospital promoted itself as "A Hospital for mental and nervous disorders in persons of the private class only".

It also promoted the fact that it had "excellent and modern treatment for all types of mental disorders".

In its prospectus the Hospital is described as being of high quality and in pleasant surroundings. Any patient looking southward over the gardens would see just trees and fields. The two roads either side of the Hospital, Church Lane and Upton Lane were at that time country lanes winding through open fields and farms. The Hospital was effectively in the countryside.

Equally, the view from the north, side though not so attractive showed the Hospital's farm fields stretching away towards Chosen Hill with little evidence of housing.

It was stressed in the prospectus that the Hospital's voluntary Committee of Management gained 'no pecuniary advantage' and all surplus funds were ploughed back into the Hospital for the advantage and comfort of the patients. Such facilities as the Skittle Alley, Concert Hall and fine gardens were given as examples. The farm was also promoted as being able to supply fresh produce to the Hospital.

Barnwood House Hospital was intended for two classes of patient:

Firstly, "Patients in more or less affluent circumstances, who shall contribute, according to the accommodation required, such sums as may be agreed upon."

Secondly, "Patients in limited circumstances, but in a position in life to render them unsuitable for admission into County Asylums".

Having fulfilled these conditions, they would be accepted at reduced rates of payment if they satisfied these three requirements,

1. They must possess so much education or refinement as would cause them to feel the loss of comfortable surroundings.
2. They must, from want of means be unable to pay the ordinary rate.
3. Their mental condition must be such as to show a reasonable prospect of recovery.

There were three ways a patient could be admitted.

1. Voluntarily. These were patients needing treatment, who were able to sign an admission form, and could leave, giving 72 hours notice.

2. On a Temporary basis. These patients were Incapable of answering "are you willing to undergo treatment?" They could be admitted for up to six months.

3. Certified. Patients in this category were admitted following a legal process confirming insanity.

The prospectus goes on to advise,

"The friends of patients should send with them a good supply of the clothing which they usually wear, marked with the full name.

No razors, knives, scissors, or other dangerous articles, or money or other valuables should be sent.

It is very desirable that when patients are bought to the Hospital, they should not, if it can possibly be avoided, be deceived as to their destination. Such deception always produces an injurious effect afterwards."

The Hospital's Ethos

Being a private institution, managed by a board of trustees, patients were expected to pay for their accommodation and treatment. However, admission was based solely on social needs and mental condition, and not on the ability to pay.

Thus, patients were subsidised provided that they "possessed so much education and refinement as would cause them to feel the loss of comfortable surroundings if they were to be sent to less luxurious accommodation". "They must, from want of means, be unable to pay the ordinary rate and their mental condition must be such as to show a reasonable prospect of recovery." (This latter constraint was a legal requirement on the trustees to ensure funds were appropriately spent.)

Preference for financial assistance was given to those patients who came from, or were associated with, the County of Gloucestershire.

Those directly involved with the care and welfare of patients were required to read and follow the Hospital's Rule Book. Being very comprehensive, it would have been updated over the years, though the fundamentals would have not changed since they were drawn up in 1866 in conjunction with the Commissioners for the Insane.
Here are some of its directives.

Because they are insane, the patients are not to be treated with less respect than they would be entitled to if they were of sound mind and at liberty.

They are not the less ladies and gentlemen because they are unsound in mind.

Head Attendants 'They shall visit all the rooms in their departments not later than seven o'clock every morning, and see that the Attendants and Nurses are up, and attending to their duty, that the bedroom windows are opened and that the patients are washed and neatly dressed before breakfast.'

'They shall pay a second visit after prayers, when they shall inspect the rooms and beds, and change the newspapers and periodicals, preparatory to the visit of the Superintendent.'

'They shall always be present when a patient is forcibly fed and shall report to the Superintendent, in writing, the hour of such feeding, and the quantity and nature of the food administered.'

'They shall attend the services in the Chapel, morning and evening prayer, and the associated amusements.'

Ordinary attendants and servants 'They must not, on any account, repeat out of the Institution anything connected with it, and especially the names, history, and conduct of the patients.' [21]

'No male attendant is permitted, on any pretence, to enter the female department, nor a female that of the males, unless ordered to do so by the Superintendent; neither is any attendant allowed in the kitchen or basement between the meal-bells.'

'The attendants are to take care that the tables are neatly laid at meal times, and that the knives, forks glasses, etc., are clean and bright. These are to be carefully counted and locked up after each meal.'

'Grace is to be reverently said by the attendants before each meal, and strict order preserved.'

---

[21] This was strictly adhered to and, many years after they had left, staff who worked in the Hospital were often reluctant to talk about their time there.

The Welcoming Interior

Right from the outset, the Hospital set its standards high. It aimed to attract and cater for patients from the upper and middle classes and to make their stay there feel as homely and welcoming as possible.

Both interior and exterior were laid out and furnished in the style of the accommodation patients would be accustomed to. The furnishings were of good quality and there were plenty of day rooms and quiet places that would have been familiar to, and expected by, the patients.

The main entrance was accessed from a semi-circular drive off Barnwood Road.

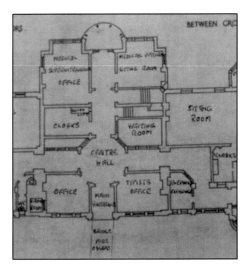

This is a plan of the ground floor showing the entrance hall which led to an ornate octagonal Central Hall.

Off this hall were the two administration offices, a cloakroom and waiting room – behind which was the Medical Superintendent's office and sitting room.

Either side were the corridors that led to more areas for visitors and beyond that into the wings of the Hospital itself.

The plan shows that doorways closed off the two wings ensuring that visitors did not wander into the wards. One of the afternoon duties of the Domestics was to escort visitors to the patients.

In this Central Hall was an ornate wooden Post Box. One postman who regularly cleared this box told me that it was a strange experience entering this hall where there would be patients standing around watching him both deliver and retrieve the mail.

Post was vetted before being handed to patients and also vetted before being placed in the post box.

Looking across the Central Hall from west to east. The houses of Cherston Court can be seen through the window.

This picture is looking from the Superintendent's office across the Central Hall, towards the entrance doors.

These pictures were taken by Robert (Robin) Morris who purchased the central block after the Hospital closed. Dated about 1971, by which time he had taken up residence and the two wings had been demolished.

The ornate nature of this tiled hall can be clearly seen and must have been given the first-time visitor quite an impression.

These two pictures of hallways have been difficult to place but are assumed to be in the ground floor visitor area. Note the rugs, and the ornaments, especially on the door pediments.

94

The following pictures, mainly publicity photographs, give an insight of what it must have been like to stay there.

Most patients had their own bedroom, although there were a few dormitories for those patients who could not afford the single room accommodation charges.

Each room had a fireplace and throughout the building there were supplementary heating radiators.

A dormitory.

From the following pictures it can be seen that some of the dining rooms for both males and females were elegant.

No.1 Male Dining Room.
Note the gentleman hiding behind the plant.

No 1 patients were not restricted for many of their activities and so could enjoy a convivial and relaxing meal in pleasant surroundings.

A Ladies' Dining Room.

The following three pictures, taken of the same Ladies' Drawing Room, show how the furniture and decoration changed over the years.

As early as 1897 the Hospital had a basic telephone system which was upgraded in 1933 to a 32-station private telephone exchange, which serviced the whole of the Hospital and its outbuildings. There was also a 'state of the art' fire alarm system which was connected to the nearby residences of all key members of the staff.

Sanitary arrangements were upgraded over the years.
Around 1882 The Hospital installed self-flushing toilets in the main toilet building at a time when toilet facilities elsewhere around the estate, were somewhat primitive.
Toilet blocks were built on the outside of the building, mainly on the north (utilitarian) side. This caused problems with pipes freezing during the cold winter months until heating was installed in them.

The Hospital was essentially long corridors with rooms off them. There were doors along these which were closed, separating the different categories of patients.

Over the years, the corridors were widened to give a less oppressive feel and extra light into the interior.

Airflow and ventilation seemed to be a problem.
An interesting and innovative system of ensuring at least the main rooms had fresh air was achieved whereby fresh air entered at floor level over coils of hot water pipes and the 'foul' air left at ceiling levels through gratings.

By 1882, fresh water was piped from the local Churchdown reservoir. This was a direct feed except to the toilet cisterns which would have been supplied from the tanks on the roof. These were fed by water pumped up from the Wotton Brook which ran through the gardens.

The Medical Staff

Over the years the relationships between the staff and the Hospital Committee were untroubled.

Care was taken in the hiring of staff, especially those involved in the care of patients. These were the patients' companions, nurses, and attendants; and there was no shortage of applicants for these positions.

The success of the Hospital was in part due to the quality and commitment of the staff. This was often mentioned in the Annual Reports.

In many instances salaries were paid on an individual basis allowing for the selection of the best qualified and most suitable person.

Long hours made boarding necessary and essential. However, this was a significant attraction to many, as it was tax free.

Superintendents

The head of the Hospital medical staff was the Medical Superintendent (Head Doctor) supported by deputies and the Hospital's Matron.

The Hospital appointed its first Head Doctor in 1858 as the building started to be converted into a hospital. He was Dr. Alfred Joshua Wood who was to serve jointly with his wife Frances Beeston Wood as Matron. Their starting salary was £300 plus board and lodging.

Frances was Alfred's 2nd wife, and their daughter married the Barnwood Worthy, Walter Bryan Wood.

Alfred's brother, Charles Fredrick Bryan Wood was vicar of Barnwood from 1841 to 1844.

Many of the Hospital's senior management were either related to each other or moved in the same social circles.

Dr. Wood established the pattern of personal care as a base for the future. Of the four hundred and fifty-one patients admitted during his fifteen-year tenure, one hundred recovered, and the daily average number grew to ninety-four.

He was succeeded in 1874, by Frederick Needham, M.D. (Later Sir Frederick Needham).

Dr. Needham continued to build on the sound foundation laid by Dr. Wood and initiated many alterations and additions to improve quality. By the time he left in 1892, the average number had grown to one hundred and sixty-two.

In the Hospital's Annual Report of 1892, the committee recorded that "To him and to the voluntary assistance of Mrs. Needham has been chiefly due to the great reputation this Hospital enjoys as one of the best in Great Britain".

Dr. Needham resigned upon being appointed as a Commissioner - an honour to the Hospital as well as to him personally.

Dr. Needham's position was then filled by James Greig Soutar, who had joined the Hospital in 1883 as Assistant Medical Officer to Dr. Needham. During the nine years as his assistant, he gained first-hand experience and so was able to take due advantage of this on his appointment as Superintendent.

His knowledge of all things relating to Barnwood House was profound. When he retired in 1918 the reputation of the Hospital was even higher, and although large sums were spent on improvement the financial position was even stronger than at the time of his appointment. His interest in Barnwood House was a dominant one, extending into his retirement. He continued his work in the field of Psychiatry and his opinion was much valued by colleagues. He was elected President of the Royal College of Psychiatry in 1912.

Following him was Arthur Allen Deykin Townsend, M.D. Before taking up the role of Superintendent, he had been an Assistant Medical Officer at Hospital since 1890 and thus had some knowledge of Dr. Needham's methods and a sound one of those of Dr. Soutar, which he was able to put to full use.

Amongst his achievements was the opening of the Manor House for voluntary boarders, the introduction of a training school for nurses and the adoption of rules for a formal pension scheme.

Throughout the nineteen years of his intendency, the Hospital retained its pre-eminent status and the invested funds steadily increased. His total years of service was a remarkable forty-seven.

To see the Hospital through difficult years, though not knowing this at that time, Gerald William Thomas Hunter Fleming was appointed in 1937. When he came to Barnwood House Dr. Fleming's reputation was already well established after wide experience in other hospitals, including the previous five years as Medical Superintendent at Hereford Mental Hospital, Burghill, and its separate branch for private patients at Holme Lacy.

One of the several other appointments he held for many years was that of Editor of the Journal of Mental Science. He was also a member of the Council of the Royal Medico-Psychological Association, of which learned society, he was elected President in 1953. He was also later Chairman of the Burden Neurological Institute. This reflected the growth of research activities being undertaken in the Hospital under his leadership.

At Barnwood House he was regarded by some of the administrative staff as a 'Toff' especially when in late 1950s, he had provided for his personal use two Daimler limousines each with a chauffeur. When it was suggested that one was enough, he retorted that two were essential in case he was called out in the night to see a possible new patient.

However, he brought a new influence on policy and achieved much. His tenure was somewhat clouded by the national crisis immediately preceding the second world war, by the war when it happened, and by the changed conditions following it.

Unfortunately, when there were mounting problems, his health gradually deteriorated, and in 1963 he collapsed and died whilst on duty.

To guide the Hospital through its final years, Thomas Eggleston Burrows. took over the reins. He was formerly Physician Superintendent at Burghill and Holme Lacy Hospitals, Hereford, and from February 1961, Deputy Medical Superintendent at Barnwood House.

Dr Burrows was much better qualified over financial matters than either Doctor Fleming or the Hospital's chairman, W. I. Croome, and he wasted no time in opening the Committee's eyes to the plight at Barnwood.

He undertook this difficult task and the burden of additional work arising from it with purpose and resource.

When the Hospital closed in 1968 the appointment of Medical Superintendent became redundant. Dr. Burrows was thus the last in a line of six Medical Superintendents of Barnwood House Hospital.

Matrons

When Barnwood House Hospital was opened, the joint appointment of Dr. and Mrs. Wood as Medical Superintendent and Matron was made. This arrangement was a common one at the time, it had advantages which could readily be seen and some disadvantages.

Living under one roof in close company, including sharing the same table for meals with patients, did much to foster the 'family home' conditions, encouraged both by the Commissioners and by the Committee.

Mrs. Wood's own contribution right from the beginning was a major and demanding one and was duly recognised.

Mrs. Needham did not hold an appointment, but as Dr. Needham's wife and resident she was favourably placed to help sustain and develop still further the same family atmosphere. The Annual Reports paid regular tribute to her services of various kinds "given gratuitously".

Miss Kate Buckle who had been a Head Attendant in Mrs. Needham's time, was appointed Matron in 1892, and her twenty-six years of service until her retirement, due to ill health, in 1918, were marked by her kindness and efficiency which became almost a legend. She died in 1923.

Miss Mable G Edwards followed Miss Buckle. She was matron for twenty years.

In 1937 Anne MacMillan, who came from the Royal Edinburgh Mental Hospital came to take charge of the gentlemen attendants. This she did with such success that when the post of matron became vacant in the following year she was selected in the face of strong opposition. In her thirty years as matron, the problems, and issues she faced were more numerous and difficult than those that had faced her predecessors. She left the Hospital when it closed in 1968.

The Nursing Staff

Whilst the Hospital had its own fully qualified medical staff it did not employ a General Practitioner. Therefore, the Local (Hucclecote) GP would be called on to attend patients and whenever a patient needed to be 'Sectioned'. [22]

Over the years, as the Hospital, and therefore staff numbers, grew a hierarchy of staffing developed.

At the top was the Head Doctor, sometimes known as the Superintendent. All the appointments were male, and they were all highly qualified. They were supported by deputies, who were called assistant Head Doctor.

There was a Matron, who had charge of the nursing staff and who reported to the Superintendent.

On the female side Matron was supported by a Head Nurse, Senior Sisters, and Sisters. There were also nurses titled 'Deputy Assistant Matron and 'Sister Tutor'.

The male side had a similar hierarchy, with Head Attendants and Deputy Head Attendants.

The titles, 'Nurse', 'Attendant' and 'Attendant on the Insane' are used throughout the records and could refer to either male or female staff. However, attendants were often qualified nurses and nurses 'attended' to their patients.

The Hospital was segregated into a male wing (west) and a female wing (east), and the rules specifically prohibited staff from crossing wings unless requested. Even the staff rest rooms, and dining areas were separate.

---

[22] Sectioning a patient is a formal, legal process whereby a person is admitted for treatment without necessarily their formal consent.

It was a strict rule that all female staff had to be unmarried and were therefore required to leave when they married.

This did not apply to the male staff, though the long hours meant that few were married.

The picture below, is believed to show Matron Buckle with her female staff at her retirement in 1918.

It is thought, because of her demeanour and attire, that Matron Buckle is sitting to the left of the picture. Behind her could be Miss Price who left soon after to get married. She had been Head Nurse for some 15 years.

Miss Edwards, deputy to Miss Price was appointed to replace Miss Buckle. Comparing the uniforms, she could either be one of the three other nurses standing at the back, or one of the two nurses sitting near Miss Buckle.

Nursing staff lived in the Hospital alongside the patients and therefore their accommodation was better than that of many others in similar occupations. They ate what the patients ate. "If salmon was in season, then we ate salmon, if it was pheasant, then we ate pheasant", related one domestic.

From the early days, staff responsibilities towards the care of patients were clearly laid out in the Hospital's Rule Book. Typical of the tone was the introduction, with staff being reminded that "patients suffered from a disease and were therefore to be pitied and not blamed. They must be treated with the same respect as if they were of sound mind and at liberty". There were over 50 rules laying out the duties and responsibilities for the Head Attendants, Night Attendants, Ordinary Attendants and Servants. At the end, written in red, were the penalties and fines incurred for breaking these rules.

The day started early. Head Attendants had visited all the rooms in their departments by seven o'clock, when the night staff handed over to the day staff. This ensured that the attendants and nurses were up and fulfilling their duty, that bedroom windows were opened and that patients were washed and neatly dressed ready for breakfast.

Morning prayers were then said, after which there was a daily inspection. All newspapers and periodicals were changed, and the rooms cleaned and tidied.

Grace was said at mealtimes. Patients were allowed wine, and this was recorded in the 'Wine and Diet' book. Attendants were required to "neatly lay out the tables at mealtimes", cutlery and glasses were to be "clean and bright and carefully counted and locked up after each meal".

There was strict segregation between the sexes. Female patients occupied the east wing, male patients, the west. Attendants of one sex could not enter the living areas of the other unless duly instructed to do so.

At dusk during the winter and at 9pm in the summer, all external doors were locked. The night staff came on duty at 9pm. Evening prayers were followed by a general locking of internal doors preparatory to all patients being settled down by 10pm.

Every effort was made to ensure that night-time was quiet and orderly. Doors and windows were secured on windy nights to stop rattling and the staff had to wear shoes that did not make a noise on the floors. At night, special attention was given to the care of epileptic or suicidal patients to ensure that they were safe.

Attendant Jack Bishop with a patient.

Jack Bishop was an attendant on Male 4 wing. This was where some of the more serious cases were treated.

It is said that Jack would take orders from the patients for tobacco products as they could not go out and purchase these themselves.

Attendants and servants were required to ensure that any patient in their care did not run away. The cost of "retaking such a patient" would be deducted from their wages.

The story is told of a male patient who, on being apprehended as he made his escape, offered the attendant a year's salary if he would let him go. Needless to say, this offer was refused, and the patient escorted back to the Hospital.

For most of the time staffing levels were sufficient. Only during the two world wars did the Hospital have some slight difficulties.
In 1935, the 151 patients were looked after by 72 nurses, both male and female, who worked unusually long hours.
From at least 1920, both male and female nurses attend training lectures. That year a number of students took the preliminary examination of the Medical Psychological Association, twenty of these were successful.

Whilst generally being beneficial to the Hospital, it was difficult to stop junior female nurses leaving as soon as they were trained and thus becoming useful. Imposing a contract was considered to ensure this did not happen.

By 1925, the Hospital had gained a high reputation as a training school for mental nursing and so, sometime after 1926, a suitable separate building was constructed and fitted out for this purpose.

Some while after, the training course was expanded, and nurses were allowed to go for general nursing training after completing their mental training. Many who took up this additional training remained with the Hospital, for being double trained they were entitled to generous pension benefits offered by Hospital.

This double, or cross, training resulted in a beneficial close relationship with Gloucester Hospital. The commissioners, in their inspection report for 1931, commented how good staff training was as a result of this.

Research

Ever since it opened in 1860, Barnwood House Hospital had always been at the forefront of research into treatments for mental illness. But its most active period in this field was during the middle years of the 20th century.

In 1939, Barnwood House was the first hospital in this country to undertake Electroconvulsive Therapy, also known as ECT or electric shock therapy.

The pre-frontal leucotomy was tried at Barnwood House in 1941 after studying results obtained in Italy and in America.

In 1946, a research department was set up and staff engaged. The Committee attached much importance to this department not only for the advantage of their patients but as a contribution to mental health generally.

Its director, William Ross Ashby was recruited in 1947 and much research work was undertaken during the twelve years that he, a deep and original thinker, was Director of Research at the Hospital.

Initially the department's investigation focussed into the biochemistry of the brain before and after electric shock treatment and before and after the operation of prefrontal leucotomy.

Over the years, the department expanded its work, much considered to be fundamental research. Most of this was being done by the Hospital's Physician-Superintendent, Dr. Fleming, and the director of the Burden Neurological Institute, Bristol, Professor Golla.

Under Dr. Fleming's, direction the patients at Barnwood House were for many years able to receive the benefit of the most modern methods of treatment both physical and psychological.

William Ross Ashby

William Ross Ashby was born in 1903. He attended Cambridge University and eventually became a psychiatrist and a pioneer in cybernetics. During this time, he published two books, "An Introduction to Cybernetics" and "Design for a Brain", both of which were widely regarded.

It was in 1947, after serving in India with the Royal Army Medical Corps, that he came to Barnwood. Initially, as a biochemist, he was employed to investigate the enzymes involved in electro-convulsive therapy (often referred to as ECT or electric shock treatment). This process had been invented in Italy in 1938 and was first used in the UK, at Barnwood House, a year later when it was trialled on five patients.

In 1941, the Hospital became the first institution to use leucotomy as a treatment. As Director of Research, Ashby was very much involved in the development of these two techniques.

In his spare time, Ashby built his "thinking machine" using four ex-RAF bomb control units, valves, and liquid-filled, magnetically driven potentiometers. By March 1948, with assistance from his laboratory assistant, Denis Bannister, he had successfully constructed and tested his machine which he called the 'Homeostat' the name taken from the word homeostasis, a term used in biology to refer to the control of internal conditions, such as blood temperature, within a living organism.

The Homeostat became a minor sensation and was heavily featured in the popular press of the day being described variously as 'the Robot Brain' or 'The Thinking Machine'. A very private man Ashby was somewhat uncomfortable with the attention although he presented the Homeostat at conferences, most famously the ninth Macy Conference on Cybernetics (1952).

Ross Ashby with the "Homeostat".

The invention certainly created worldwide interest. It was a very heavy machine and the most advanced of its kind. In January 1949, *Time* magazine quoted Ashby as saying, "it is the closest thing to a synthetic human brain so far designed by man".

Image of the Homeostat taken from Ashby's lecture slides.

In the Ashby archives there is some correspondence between Ashby and Alun Turin regarding the processes of thinking and computation. They agreed to differ. Turin's approach was essentially 'digital' and therefore the basis of today's computer. Ashby's was 'analogue' which took a back seat over the following years.

Ross was a competent repairer of clocks and watches and whilst at Barnwood House he willingly aided those whose timepieces had malfunctioned. Occasionally, he became so preoccupied with his work that, according to the person who delivered his daily lunch to the laboratory, he would forget to eat his meal.

He was regarded by contemporaries at the Hospital as a friendly gentleman who encouraged and assisted students.

He served as Director of Research of the Barnwood House Hospital from 1947 until 1959. For a year, he was Director of the Burden Neurological Institute in Bristol.

Many of the results of his and the department's research were read in papers to various scientific societies at meetings both held at Barnwood and also far afield. Some were published in scientific publications with world-wide circulations. His work gained international status. It had already been acclaimed in the United States of America by the sponsoring of his lecture tour there in 1952 and the award by the Ford Foundation in 1955 of a research fellowship at Stanford University, California.

In 1960, he went to the United States of America and became the Professor of Biophysics and Electrical Engineering, at the University of Illinois at Urbana–Champaign, until his retirement in 1970.

Throughout the rest of his academic life and into retirement Ross Ashby continued to work on his journal, recording thoughts and ideas, and only stopping in March 1972 just three months before his death. By then his journal stretched to over 7,000 pages spread across 25 volumes.

Ross Ashby died in 1972.

One of two laboratories where Ashby worked c1955.
This is sited where the skittles would be stood at the end of the alley.

The Laboratory March 1955.
Sited in the old Billiard Room.

The Support Staff

The Hospital could not function without dedicated teams whose roles were to keep it running. Many of these teams were responsible for the regular maintenance and improvements essential for such a busy hospital and could be called on at short notice when things went wrong.

Clerical and Administrative.

To support the Head Doctor and the Hospital generally, there was a secretariat, based on the ground floor of the main building. Their office was to the right of the entrance and behind this was the telephone exchange.

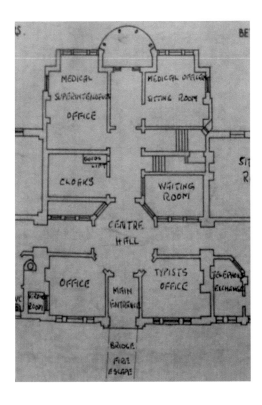

In the latter years of the Hospital this office was run by Martin Booty, Administration Officer, supported by a number of typists. Mr Booty sat in the office to the left of the entrance, with the Trust's secretary, Tom Gale.

Whilst the majority of the staff wore uniforms, the typists wore their normal clothes. This was changed about 1963 when a smart uniform was designed for them.

The following photos are from Jill Tucker, one of the admin staff, and show her and her colleagues in the Hospital's grounds after the introduction of their uniforms. Also present are Mary Wheeler and Margaret Buttling

Tom Gale with Martin Booty and his administration staff in their new uniforms.
Taken about 1963.

Domestics

Though, initially domestics lived outside the Hospital, from the 1881 census onwards records show that 'Housemaids' now lived in. The numbers were however quite small for such a big institution, five in 1881 and 1891, seven in 1901, nine in 1911 and thirteen plus a Head Housemaid in 1939. It could therefore be that these were the 'core' who lived in and were there at the start of the Hospital's day to be supplemented by staff that came in later.

In 1911 there was also a needlewoman, five laundry maids and two scullery maids.

Twelve-year-old Sidney Birches was living there in 1901, as a Pageboy. It was his job, dressed smartly in his uniform, to greet visitors as they arrived at the main entrance. Ten years later, Albert Blake, who was 15, was the Hospital's Pageboy.

In the latter years the Domestics wore blue and white uniforms in the morning and black and white after lunch, when visitors were welcomed and escorted to the patients.

Porters and Labourers

One group essential to the smooth running of the Hospital were the porters and general labourers.

In January 1910, either because clarification was needed or there were new appointments, two handwritten documents were produced, one setting out the duties and responsibilities of the Porter and the other for two Labourers.

These give an interesting insight into two overlapping roles which were essential for the smooth running of the Hospital's infrastructure.

The porter mentioned in the document was R Berry, and one of the two labourers was W Bircher.

Quite how many porters and labourers the Hospital employed is a matter of conjecture but would have fluctuated over the years as needs arose and fell.

There was a clear demarcation of tasks between these men, the porter being the more senior, but for certain tasks they worked as a team.

The porter was 'to clean all Ladies' and Gentlemen's boots and shoes. Collecting and returning to gents lockers only'. [No male was allowed in the female wings without permission.] The two labourers were 'to assist the porter, when necessary, to clean boots and wash the basement pavements.'

The porter was required to 'collect from different parts of the house all linen for the labourers to take to and from the laundry returning the laundry when clean'.

The laundry was originally in the basement before it moved to the area by the boiler house, it would seem laundry was placed there by the attendants and collected by the porter.

An interesting task entrusted to the porter was the cleaning of all knives [but not forks] counting them and placing them back in boxes for each of the rooms. [An important task then as it would be today for it was essential to ensure no patient had the tools with which to self-harm or to inflict injury on another. Every knife had to be accounted for.]

Given the restriction in going into the ladies wing it could be assumed that each dining room had a box for cutlery which was replenished in the basement as the utensils used in each meal were washed.

In this list of duties, we see reference to the storekeeper, one of those seldom mentioned roles but essential to the smooth running of the kitchen and Hospital.

The porter was 'to assist the Storekeeper to tap all beer and wines and spirits and unpacking and the cutting up of stored meat.

He was also required to 'salting and otherwise curing bacon, hams etc fetching and weighing in same to kitchen'. (Later the curing of bacon was undertaken in a purpose-built building on the farm.)

More akin to the porter's tasks we would expect today was the requirement to 'transferring luggage to and from box room, taking and fetching all parcels and luggage to and from stations and town shopping generally' [Gloucester had two railway stations at that time, and it is also possible that Cheltenham's three stations were also used. This begs the question as the whether he did this by public transport, Hospital cart/carriage and if the latter, did he require the use of a coachman?

The instructions also covered their responsibilities as regards cleaning. The porter's responsibilities were mainly internal – 'cleaning windows fitting, coal boxes scouring basement floors, assisting to spring clean etc'. Whilst the labourers were mainly responsible for outside - 'to cleanse and keep in order, inside and outside all drains, cesspools, spoutings, flats, areas etc. To clean all windows externally. To take down gratings and keep clean radiators pipes etc. To wash and keep clean all outside doors gates urinals and cesspools.'

Again, an interesting insight into the trades employed by the Hospital, for the labourers were 'to assist carpenters in repairing fences etc to grounds to assist the different tradesmen inside and outside the House. To keep clean workshops yard etc stack timber and assist tradesmen generally.'

Regular duties involved 'stacking and otherwise trimming(?) coal in cellars and breaking same for porter to fill into boxes. To fix and keep in order the tennis nets, cricket screens etc. To beat and clean carpets.'

There was no opportunity for slacking as the labourers were also required 'during wet weather to whitewash corridors and various offices in the basement'.

The Maintenance Team

All staff were forbidden to smoke inside the building, and they were expected to be always sober and well-attired. Indeed, this picture of the maintenance team clearly shows the majority wearing jackets and ties.

The maintenance staff in the late 1950s.

Back Row: Joe Hodgetts (odd jobs), Charlie McBurnie (engineer), Tom Morgan (plumber and handyman), Wilf Halliday, and others.

Front row, (a painter/carpenter), Bert Smith (Clerk of Works), Bill Parry (chauffer).

The Chief Engineer.

About 1930 the Hospital decided to employ a fulltime engineer who was permanently on site to maintain the ever-growing numbers of mechanical devices the Hospital needed day to day for its efficient operation. He was Robert Peckham, a Railway Engineer.

On the death of his father, Robert left the Hospital and moved to his parent's home in Tadworth, sometime around 1945

The position of Chief Engineer was then given to Charles McBurnie. Initially employed as the Hospital's stoker, maintaining the boilers both within the laundry and also those in the basement of the Hospital itself. He moved with his wife from 'Garden Cottage' alongside The Manor House, into 'Engineer's Cottage' where he would remain until the Hospital closed some twenty years later.

His background was with machines, having started his career in the mills of Bolton, moving to the naval shipyards of Chatham and Portsmouth when the mills closed.

The role of chief engineer seems to have been a wide ranging one, and he was seen as a very useful member of the support staff. His residence on Hospital grounds enabled him to attend to both the trivial and important at all hours of the day and night.

Typical of an 'important task' would be the fixing of the Head Doctor's television when it went wrong.

Barnwood House Fire Brigade

During the 1930s there was a rush to reorganise the country's fire fighters. Until this time there had been no nationwide policy and local authorities had made their own arrangements. With the likelihood of a future aerial war increasing, more appliances were manufactured and a number of these were purchased by private organisations wishing to provide their own cover. One such body was Barnwood House Hospital.

The private brigade was manned by volunteers drawn from the staff of the Hospital and they took delivery of a Dennis Trailer Pump on 23rd June 1937. It cost the princely sum of £636 and was stored in the Hospital garage. Formerly the stables, this building still stands on Barnwood Road, almost opposite Cherston Court, and is easily recognised by its clock tower.

Duties included protecting the Hospital and training the staff to cope with fires.

The new crew did not have to wait long for their first emergency call. It came on 26th August 1937 when a hay rick caught fire. The incident took place in a field behind Avenue Cottage, which still stands on the main road opposite Barnwood Avenue. In those days this land formed part of the Hospital farm.

The crew pulled and pushed the pumping appliance down Barnwood Road as fast as they could. But it was unbalanced and so they persuaded a 10-year-old lad named John Morris to sit on the pump and act as ballast. John Morris took little persuading. Over seventy years later he recalled the occasion and remembered the excitement. The Brigade logbook reports being "called out at 4.20pm". Water was "pumped from a disused gravel pit at 110 lbs per square inch for half an hour. Hayrick controlled and fire prevented from spreading to barn nearby". The emergency was resolved "by 5.30pm and 550 feet of hose was used".

A somewhat amusing incident happened that afternoon. A well-known local gentleman went to watch the new brigade in action and some of his comments directed towards the crew became offensive; he was put in his place by a well-aimed jet of water from the hose!

Such call outs were rare. The crew spent the war years supervising the Hospital air raid shelters and, night after night, taking the pump engine to the brook and laying out the hoses for the anticipated air attack. Fortunately, it never came; the nearest bomb fell a few hundred yards away from the Hospital.

After the war, the crew took delivery of a new appliance. A Sulzer pump engine.

This significantly repaired picture shows the Barnwood House crew in the mid-1950s, after they had joined the AFS, standing in front of the Fordson. The words "Trustees of Barnwood House" can be deciphered on the side of the appliance. The two men on the extremes are instructors from the AFS; the central six are from the Hospital. Left to right they are Tom Morgan, Wilf Halliday, Cliff Porter, Bill Morris, Ron Baldwin and Charlie McBurnie

The Barnwood House Brigade enlisted with the Auxiliary Fire Service (AFS) and, for a while at least, one of the Bedford Green Goddesses was entrusted to their care. By this time the emphasis was on Civil Defence training as the nation prepared itself for the possibility of a nuclear attack. Fire drill no longer took place at the Hospital but at the fire station on Barnwood Road and later at Eastern Avenue.

The crew regularly practised at the docks on the fire launch "Salamander" and competed as an AFS team in fire service competitions.

Coincidentally, both the Hospital and the AFS ceased to exist in 1968, the former because of financial difficulties, the latter because of the receding risk of nuclear attack.

A Day to Remember

Whilst this actual story is fictitious it reflects many of the tasks and activities that went on.

'Word got round quickly. There was steam leaking from the tunnel that went past the tennis courts and under the main road. It was the tunnel that ran from the boiler house on the north side to the main building on the south side of the road. The pipes were not in ideal condition and leaks occurred regularly. It was important to repair it because it conveyed heat to the Hospital. The first person with a bit of clout to hear the news would ring four or five chaps from the maintenance unit who were not otherwise engaged: that would be their afternoon accounted for. There would need to be at least an engineer, a plumber and a couple of others who were not involved in any other emergency. So that could mean stokers, painters, porters, chauffeurs, engineers, carpenters, plumbers, and the sparks - almost twenty in all. They would be contacted on the state-of-the-art telephone network which ran across the estate. There were fewer than one hundred receivers in the system and so there were fewer than one hundred numbers to remember - and only two digits each. After a week you knew the lot.

It was no good ringing the porters as at least two of them were busy loading the litter, rubbish, and waste into the large-wheeled handcart in order to push, and sometimes pull, across from the main building to the incinerator which was next to the boiler house. This was a daily (sometimes twice) occurrence. The chauffeur was already out for the day taking the Medical Superintendent off to an important meeting at Hume Towers in Bournemouth. All the painters were painting Number 2 Ladies Dining Room. The stokers were needed to shovel on the coal in the boiler house as the building was still years before becoming oil fired. The Electrician was on holiday. So that left the two carpenters to give a hand to the engineer and the plumber in the tunnel. And the repair wasn't finished until half past seven in the evening. Happy days.'

(By Brian McBurnie who grew up in the Hospital grounds.)

Christmas at the Hospital

Christmas at the Hospital was always well celebrated. Each ward would have its own very tall Christmas tree which had been supplied from the Hospital grounds. It was tastefully decorated and was the focus of the ward party. Staff, and children from the Hospitals' estate, were invited to these occasions and, indeed, encouraged to attend as it was considered beneficial to the patients' wellbeing. A big cake would be cut, and delicacies would be offered on large silver trays. Crackers would be pulled, and the ward sister would deliver a short seasonal message.

As Christmas approached, the choirs from both Hucclecote Parish Church and Barnwood Church attended in order to entertain the patients.

A former Hucclecote chorister recalled that "we changed into our cassocks and surplices in a billiard room just off the main corridor. We were then ushered into a large hall and went through our repertoire of carols. I can remember feeling rather apprehensive when faced with rows of residents some of whom did seem rather different and displayed some odd behaviour. However, this was all made well worthwhile when we were each given half a crown for our efforts. It seemed like a lot of money to us in those days. My overriding memory of the place was of rather splendid decor and fittings, with lots of very high ceilings and highly polished wood."

Barnwood Church choir sang in the main hallway and corridors. One chorister recounted "at the Hospital we never saw any patients; we were led down several wide and well-furnished corridors and sang in hallways close to open doors. The sound travelled well, and the nursing staff seemed to appreciate it. We were always on our best behaviour; it was clearly expected, and the place had the sort of atmosphere where everyone felt obliged to behave anyway. But it was really Christmassy, singing around the Christmas trees."

It was a very busy time for both nurses and domestic staff with little time off and much rushing around. But they were well rewarded with a "magnificent Christmas Dinner" as one former member of staff described it. She added "and you could help yourself to as much as you wanted for over the Christmas period we were really fed well; food was very, very available".

Indeed, it was, fifty Norfolk Black turkeys were supplied by the farm and, for those for whom turkey meat had little appeal, a couple of dozen capons.

The estate also produced hams for special meat teas, and there was plenty of fresh cream to top the sweet course as the cows were, understandably, still milked at Christmas.

Some of the domestic and nursing staff enjoy Christmas lunch together in 1962.
Matron is in the centre of the picture

Feeding The Hospital

The Hospital's kitchens were large and well equipped. They were underground and were part of the service area whose long underground tunnel ran from one end of the main building to the other. It was wide enough and tall enough to allow staff, goods, and services to move from one part of the Hospital to another freely and rapidly.

Attendants were only allowed to use this area at mealtimes where they had their own dining rooms and relaxation areas.

It would seem that right from the start in 1860, the Hospital's kitchens were underground, making use of the 'good wine and beer cellar' of David Walter's house.

However, it was not long before the kitchens were not big enough, and in 1890 they were refitted.

Around this time a gradual improvement in this underground area was undertaken. The kitchen walls were tiled, and the two boilers replaced. These were coal fired boilers, and one can only imagine the dirt and dust they caused to this underground area. The construction of a boiler house to the north of the Hospital to be the main supplier of hot water eventually allowed these boilers to be replaced and the laundry service to move away from this area.

By 1919 the kitchen range again needed replacing and a gas fired range was installed. The steam cooker was also upgraded. However, in 1928, when the Hospital was connected to the mains electricity supply, the cookers were replaced with electric ones.

Above the kitchens was the domestics' accommodation block which was built in 1895. The entrance drive swung behind this accommodation block and as there were windows that looked down into the kitchens, visitors to the Hospital could view the activities there.

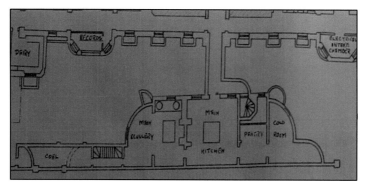

The kitchen and connecting tunnel.

Cooks and Catering Staff

The basement kitchen was the province of all those in the preparation of the Hospital's meals.

The staff were overseen by the Head Cook and here we find, in the various census records, a range of job titles. There were cooks, kitchen maids, pantry boys, pantry maids, pastry boys and pastry maids.

During the 1950s and 1960s most of the cooks were Italians from Milan and were managed by Miss 'Lena' French, a firm Scot. who was Head Cook for almost 30 years.

All staff were residential, the majority living in the three-story domestic accommodation above the Kitchen.

On hot summer days, the Italian cooks could be seen leaning out of the windows chatting to each other in true Mediterranean style.

The Italian Connection

Ever since it opened, Barnwood House had always enjoyed stability in its staffing.

Even during wartime, because of the national system for reservation of certain occupations, very few of the Hospital's staff were actually away on military service. Nevertheless, by the late 1940s, staff retirements and the availability of more attractive employment opportunities elsewhere, particularly for women, meant that there was quite a large turnover of staff. Although accommodation (there were over thirty houses on the estate) was available for maintenance staff and full board in the main building was granted to both nurses and "domestics", recruitment became an issue.

No longer could the local area supply all those needed and so, like many other organisations throughout the land, the Hospital began to look further afield.

Four kitchen staff came from Iceland and a good many more from Italy.

Female workers were only allowed to remain at the Hospital so long as they were single.
But it was a good life; they were well looked after, and they ate the same high-quality food as the patients.

Typical of the domestic staff working at the Hospital was Lucia Rubicco. She was born in Pietradefusi in southern Italy and came to the UK in 1960. Initially, she was given permission to stay for 12 months, and her residence in the UK was subject to her reporting for work at Barnwood House.
She was joined by several more domestics from her area of Italy, the majority, like her, being cooks.

Kitchen staff at work c1960.

Winter 1962, enjoying the novelty of snow; the Italian domestic staff outside the Hospital in Barnwood Road. The excitement is, apparently, because they came from a part of Italy that very rarely saw snow.

Whilst at the Hospital Lucia met and married a Ukrainian which, of course, meant that she lost her post at the Hospital. Like many other foreign domestics, she remained in the United Kingdom; indeed, some of the Italian staff and their families still live in Gloucester.

Lucia before leaving Barnwood House for her wedding at St Peter's Church. On her right is the Head Cook, Lena French, and on her left is the Hospital Matron, Anne MacMillan.

I am grateful to Lesley, Lucia's daughter for the story of her mother, and her permission to use this and the pictures of her and her colleagues. It was a chance conversation that bought these to light and the realisation by Lesley that daily, without knowing it, that she had travelled by bus past the place where her mother worked.

Many people I talk to these days have no idea what lay behind the walls along Barnwood Road and how big and significant the Hospital was.

The Hospital Farm

The Hospital had its own farm, with cattle, poultry, pigs, and cornfields. Along with its extensive market garden and greenhouses this was capable of supplying most of the Hospital's needs.

As far back as the year 1880 the committee had been concerned at the serious deterioration occurring through the neglect of the farmer to whom the land was leased. As a result, they engaged a bailiff to farm the land so that it would be within their control. This was John Rheam. Some expenditure was then required on repairing the farm buildings and draining the land.

By then milk was of sufficient quality that it could be used in the Hospital to replace the beer being supplied to patients.

1884 saw extensive additions to the farm buildings, and a year later, two cottages were built for farm workers.

The farm continued to expand. In 1890 more land was purchased with the construction of a piggery for 40 pigs.

1897 saw the construction of a house for the farm bailiff, a dairy and a bacon curing house. (Bacon being previously cured in the Hospital basement)

In 1899 the stables for the farm cart horses were replaced, and this expansion of buildings and the purchase of equipment and general improvement continued for the next couple of years.

By 1907 the Farm was able to supply the Hospital with all its potatoes and milk and most of its bacon, butter, poultry, and eggs. Expansion of its poultry farm was planned, and the kitchen garden expanded.

Additional poultry sheds and runs were constructed

It was noted in the Annual reports that when John Rheam retired in 1913 due to ill health, he had been bailiff for over 31 years and during that time his wife had done all the farm milking. Rheam died the following year and in recognition of her loyal service his widow was awarded 10/- a week pension.

The last Bailiff was Ernest Shipley.

Ernest Shipley.
The last Bailiff Farmer for the Hospital.

A drawing of the Bailiff's House.
(Artist unknown.)

One expense at the time was the re-excavation of the drinking pools and the construction of a paved path to the Horsebere Brook. The reports of 1935 comment that the brick farm bridge over the Horsebere was repaired implying that this path went some way up the hill. Subsequently, in 1956 the 1/3 mile of Horsebere brook running through farmland was improved to reduce flooding.

The impact of the first World war started to be felt by 1916 when some of the farmhands were called up for service. As a result, 3 women were employed to replace men who had left. The purchase of an engine driven elevator to assist with harvest gathering was recorded as being 'of great service'.

Expansion of the farm's poultry breeding pens continued, and two soldiers joined the depleted farm staff for part of the year to assist.

An interesting insight into the quality that the Hospital's kitchens required was that as butter was in short supply, they were unable to obtain their usual Irish Butter and no suitable local alternative was available.

So more dairy cattle were purchased, and the consumption of the farm milk reduced so that the farm could meet this butter shortfall.

After the war it the poultry farm became unsatisfactory, so most of the stock was sold, and the buildings altered. A trained ex-serviceman was appointed to take charge and the poultry farm was reconstructed, the result being 'entirely satisfactory'.

In 1921, W Parry the farm's cowman retired after 30 years' service to the Hospital.

Swine fever hit the farm in 1924 and although stringent measures were taken to minimise the impact, 23 pigs died.

By now the farm was some 300 acres in total, the two Cart Horses were disposed of, and a tractor purchased in their place. A further 12 acres were purchased in 1932, and in 1935 the 22 acres of Hill View Farm were purchased. This latter purchase reflected the desire for the Hospital's Management to resist encroachment, for the farm intersected Trust land.

During the Second World War, with food of many sorts being in short supply and some of it frugally rationed there was, as well as the vegetables and fruit from the kitchen gardens, an especially valuable bonus in the form of milk, butter, eggs poultry bacon and pork, fresh from the Hospital's farm. Even so, restrictions imposed in war time meant that there could be no real abundance for the Hospital during its duration.

During the 1950s, the farm supplied to the Hospital, two churns of fresh milk every morning and another two in the evening; each churn held ten gallons. Ten dozen eggs were delivered to the kitchen every day by the poultry man. A gallon of fresh cream was also supplied daily.

Special occasions were acknowledged with the occasional treat, for example several geese would be delivered for Michaelmas.

1955 saw the cowshed being rearranged so that the cows were tail to tail rather than head-to-head. This to simplify cleaning the shed.

But the farm was to see major alterations. The planned Barnwood bypass would cut across the farmland, cutting it into three, resulting in the loss of the best land. The dairy herd was therefore moved to land close to the farm buildings. This picture shows the cows coming home for milking.

The Herdsman is probably Freddy Waring.

The Trust now started to look at selling off some of its farmland, especially that zoned for industrial use.

Meanwhile, life continued on the farm much as before, an Increase in poultry required a deep litter house to be constructed, its dairy cattle win prizes, though one cow was fatally struck by lightning.
The success of the dairy herd meant that the farm could now sell its surplus milk.

Soon after the sale of the Hospital in 1969, the Farm was closed, and its animals and effects auctioned off by Bruton Knowles.

The Gardens

It is thought that most of the landscaping of the Hospital's grounds was done in the time of David Walters (1852), with the planting of some unusual tree varieties, many of which still exist today. Most of the mature trees are therefore now more than 150 years old.

This picture shows the grounds about 1891, after the western end of the Hospital had been extended

However, it is said that over the years, grateful patients and their families often gave the Hospital trees, many of which are not native to the UK. By the end, the collection attracted a tree preservation order, a restriction that certainly had an influence on the future of this area.

The original walled kitchen garden was reserved as an airing ground for the Hospital's ladies and a separate area was enclosed with a paling as a "court for the more excited gentlemen patients".

A bridge was built near the weir so that patients could do a circular walk, returning via a bridge further east.

Over the years the Hospital's Trust purchased land, both partly as a buffer against possible disturbances from unsuitable neighbours and partly as an investment.

Some of the land was taken up with pleasure grounds of lawns and flower beds. Recreation areas included tennis courts, croquet lawns a cricket field and gravelled walks, one of which was referred to as the 'ladies' mile'. This went around the periphery and was about a mile long, crossing the Wotton Brook via two footbridges, one over, or near the weir, the other to the east of the grounds, where the entrance to Cherston Court is today. The line of the original path can still be seen near the weir on the park side of the brook, where there is an obvious dip in the grass.

An early picture of the croquet lawn

The vista to the south from the rooms at the front of the Hospital took in the neat lawns and flower beds, the several shrubberies and spinneys of specimen evergreen and deciduous trees. It included a glimpse of the chapel through the sequoias across the stream with the cricket ground in the parkland beyond. This pleasing panorama was a delight to behold.

In contrast the other side of the building looked over the main road, the farm buildings, and fields. Churchdown Hill could be seen in the distance. This was the side which faced the outside world, and to passers-by possibly gave the impression of a very unattractive institution.

On the North side of Barnwood Road there was an area of land alongside North Cottage which was the Kitchen Garden which was used for growing vegetables.

Opposite, on the south side of the road, there was about 2½ acres, between the end of the Hospital and Manor Gardens, which was used for flowers and fruit, some of it walled and most of it sheltered, sloping to the south and there bordered by the brook.

By the early 1960s, there were 7 heated greenhouses; 7 sets of cold frames; 2 temporary greenhouses and a potting shed.

There were orchards of soft and hard fruit. It seems that this area had been set aside for an orchard and vegetable garden since the days when the house was occupied by the Walters family.

These areas were sufficiently large to easily supply the Hospital with its needs, especially during the privations of the Second World War, and over the years, the surplus produce was sold to the local community.

As the Hospital building expanded it increased the number of conservatories and day rooms, each of which had to be supplied with freshly cut flowers, which were grown in the greenhouses.

In 1894 the plant house was increased in size, and 1898 saw a house being built for the Head Gardener to replace the dilapidated cottage he then occupied. This might have been G Walker who was Head Gardener and worked for the Hospital since about 1891 and served the Hospital for some 29 years.

1907 saw an expansion of the kitchen garden, and in 1909 a new greenhouse was erected in the gardens of Manor House. The same year four hotbeds were constructed.

In 1920 F Berry, a gardener for 44 years retired. He was typical of many of the Hospital's gardening staff who served for many years.

Head Gardener, Walker, was followed in 1921 by Henry John Baldwin, then aged about 32. Baldwin was born in 'Gardener's Cottage' at the Hospital's Wilderness site, where his father Arthur James Baldwin had been the Head Gardener there since about 1884. Henry assisted his father, and as a boy of 14, is formally recorded as gardener there in the 1901 census. When the Wilderness closed in 1920, Arthur Baldwin retired after 36 years with the Hospital. This closure and retirement may have prompted the appointment of his son Henry, who would have been an experienced gardener known to the Hospital, to fill the vacancy left by Walker.

Henry and his family lived in the Hospital's Head Gardener's Cottage which was alongside the glasshouses at the eastern end of the Hospital's grounds.

This picture is of Henry John Baldwin and his son Ron at their house, Garden Cottage, 156/8 Barnwood Road

After his retirement the family moved into Hucclecote.

This shows a glasshouse at the far east of the building with the accommodation for F4 patients alongside it.

Henry Baldwin prided himself on the variety of excellent grapes that were grown in the greenhouses. The quality was such that in 1931 the Hospital won 1st Prize at the Shrewsbury Show for black grapes; first prize for Madresfield Court grapes; and third prize for Hamburghs. He also won first and third prize for scarlet flesh and green flesh melons.

First Prize.

Second prize at Shrewsbury in 1949.

In addition, some 12 gardeners were employed to maintain the lawns and flowerbeds.

The gardeners.
On the far right is Ernest Newcombe, who died in 1944.

Unexpected hazards often beset these men for it is told that, on one occasion when the lawnmower was being used, a naked female patient ran and lay down in front of the machine. Unperturbed, the gardener gently lifted the lady to one side and carried on mowing only to be faced with the same obstruction a few moments later! Attendants were soon on the scene, the lady was removed, and the gardener continued on his way.

During the outbreak of the First World War, by 1916 all the young men had left the gardening team. But with the assistance of three boys, and overtime being worked the garden remained productive and in good order.

The Wotton Brook ran through the grounds and widened into a small lake, which was held back by a weir and sluice gates, before the outflow ran under Church Lane. The lake, home to a number of swans, was never really deep enough to make drowning easy but, nevertheless, it was a target for the number of patients who had to be unceremoniously removed from its muddy waters.

The pond with swans.

Two views of the bridge over the brook.

The lower picture shows the ornamentation of the ironwork of the bridge.

A stone-built summer house and an Italian rock garden, built in 1926, offered patients a tranquil moment amongst the trees.

The summer house and rock garden with the conservatory of the Occupational Therapy room on the left.

Another view of the Occupational Therapy Room.

At the other end of the grounds, at the west end, could be seen the extension that initially contained the Skittle Alley and Billiards Room but after about 1945, the Library and Research Laboratories.

The Western extension where the laboratories and library were.

The Arboretum

When the Hospital's remaining central block was demolished in 2000, one condition placed on the builder of the houses that were erected on the site was that its grounds, which stretched down to the brook, were to be given to Gloucester City Council.

As a result, the Council rebuilt the pedestrian access bridge from the park and formed the Arboretum.

A grant from English Nature of £60,000 enabled the space to be transformed from a private garden to a Local Nature reserve and Arboretum within the now expanded Barnwood Park and it was opened as such in June of 2002 by the City Mayor (Pam Tracy) and City Sherriff (Paul James).

144

Today this area is managed by the Friends of Barnwood Arboretum working in conjunction with Gloucester City Council. Although much overgrown, the Hospital's flowerbeds and summerhouse foundations can be still discerned.

Today, the entrance to the Arboretum

A recent view towards the bridge,
taken from a property that is built on the site of the house.

The Barnwood House Estate

The Hospital's estate started with just one house and some outbuildings, all within about 42 acres.

Eventually, at its closure, some 100 years later, the Barnwood estate was about 700 acres in size, with numerous buildings and a very productive farm.

The Hospital's management also purchased lands and buildings away from Barnwood for housing both patients and staff.

This section details the evolution of those lands and buildings, the people who worked and lived there and how the estate was disposed of during the Hospital's final years.

It is no exaggeration to say that the Hospital grew in leaps and bounds, especially in the early days, as the demands of treating ever increasing numbers of patients necessitated the construction of additional bedrooms, day rooms and support facilities.

The estate also reflected this growth as more and more lands were purchased, and many support and utility buildings were constructed to support the farm and other activities.

The Hospital buildings, as seen in the picture below, eventually stretched from Church Lane in the west to Manor House at the corner of Upton Lane in the east. Service buildings were mainly to the north, whilst to the south of the Hospital the grounds were laid out to gardens, lawns, tennis courts, and a summer house. The cricket pitch and chapel were further south across the brook.

The Hospital from the southwest. The farm buildings are on the left and the boiler house and its chimney are at the top of the picture. Barnwood Road runs immediately behind the Hospital buildings.

The southern aspect with its long drive down to the brook, pleasure gardens and an uninterrupted view southward was always considered to be the front of the building, the northern aspect, the back.

This picture of the northern aspect of the Hospital from Barnwood Road, shows the domestic quarters and, to the left the head doctor's accommodation

The drive swung in from Barnwood Road and passed underneath the bridge joining the domestic annexe to the main building.

Here visitors could dismount and would be welcomed by a suitably dressed pageboy.

These two pictures show the vehicular openings in the wall.

It is just possible to see that one is one labelled 'IN', the other 'OUT'.

IN

OUT

Looking towards Hucclecote. this is a recent view of the boundary wall. The pillars of where 'IN' and 'OUT' would have been, are clearly visible.

The north side of the Hospital would have presented a rather dour and maybe daunting appearance for it was seen as being functional and therefore was never made to look attractive.

As the years progressed, additional toilets and storerooms were added to this cold north facing side, many of which, in the early days, suffered from lack of heating.

This aerial view, taken during late 1950 or early 1960, shows the hospital and the lands to the north of the main road. Welveland lane can be seen, left centre, running up the picture.

By 1935, the Hospital estate had finished growing in Barnwood. The main Hospital building was as large as it would ever be, and the farm and support buildings owned by the Hospital to the north of the main road were well established.

The map, below, shows the estate, the proposed bypass and link road that would impact the farmlands to the north, dividing them into three.

At this time, the land to be occupied by Walls' Factory has been sold by the Trustees so is not coloured.

The green coloured area to the south of Barnwood Road shows the extent of the Hospital's lands. It is believed that the southern edge of this is the boundary between Cony Hill Hospital lands and those of Barnwood.

The Other Side of the Road

Typical of the concern that the Hospital showed for the quality of the environment for its patients, all the utilitarian buildings were placed as far away from the Hospital as possible, on the grounds to the north of the main road.

The Farm and its outbuildings such as cowsheds, pig sties, chicken runs, and barns were close to Welveland Lane. To the east of these were, eventually, the Isolation Hospital (Sanitorium), the Laundry and the adjacent Boiler House.

The laundry was originally in the Hospital itself, with water supplied from the tanks at the top of the two towers either side of the central block.
The water in these was pumped up from the Wotton Brook using a ram pump. [23]

However, as the Hospital grew, this laundry could not cope and a larger, more efficient one was built in 1880 on the land to the north of the Hospital.

It was the porter's and labourer's duties each morning to handcart the dirty washing from the Hospital and return with clean laundry which they then stacked away ready for use.

Heating and hot water for the Hospital was initially supplied from six coal fired boilers in its basement, but these soon became unable to support its ever-expanding needs, and so, in 1897 an up-to-date boiler house with two coal-fired boilers was constructed alongside the Laundry. It supported both the boiler in the Laundry and supplement the needs of the Hospital with both steam and hot water.

---

[23] Ram pumps are a clever device which use the flow of water to activate the pumping mechanism.

This was a great improvement for the Hospital for it was now no longer necessary to stoke the six coal fired boilers in the basement, thus making this area much cleaner.

[At this time the central block was being rebuilt and so this upgrade to the hot water and heating made good sense.]

The initial plans for the new boiler house (referred to as the Central Power Station) were to include an electric generator. This did not materialise; the plans being considered as being not cost effective. At that time the cable supplying mains electricity from Gloucester had not yet reached Barnwood so the Hospital used gas lighting, which was considered to be very gloomy, and used generators and batteries for its electrical needs.

Soon after the construction of the boiler house, the equipment in the Laundry was refitted with better drying facilities and equipment. Several additional storage rooms were also built. During this disruption staff had to work extra hours to keep the Laundry operational.

As part of this development, a service tunnel was constructed underneath Barnwood Road, containing the pipes that led to the main building from the boiler house.

Crossing from north to south and about 30 metres to the east of the pedestrian crossing near Cherston Court, it was just high enough and wide enough for access purposes.

Quite possibly still there today running deep underneath the road and into the lands to the north.

Its southern entrance, clearly marked on the plans of the Hospital basement is now lost underneath the houses and gardens of the new estate. Its northern entrance may have been lost during the construction in about 1974 of the offices now on that site.

Initially there were two large coal fired boilers

This picture, about 1957, shows the coal fired boilers, which were installed about 1896.

Even though these boilers were a great improvement they were eventually insufficient and in 1912, a third coal fired boiler was added.

However, by 1958 these needed replacement, and so in 1960, three state of the art, oil fired units, were installed.

A twice, sometimes three times a week, delivery of oil thus commenced, the large oil tanker winding its way up the path from Barnwood Road.

These pictures show the boilers and the state-of-the-art control panel.

Regular maintenance of the chimney was carried out by steeplejacks. It is related that, to reach the top, the steeplejack had to lean backwards for the last ten feet or so, as the chimney widened at the top.

Many a challenge was made to the men of the Hospital's maintenance staff to emulate the steeplejacks, but as far as we know, only one ever succeeded in climbing over the top and back down to the boiler house.

In the picture, a steeplejack can be seen working at the top of the boiler house chimney; the laundry building is on the right.

Every morning, a handcart took the Hospital refuse to the incinerator which was situated nearby; half a mile to the north of this was the cesspit which was the destination for the Hospital's sewage

The Hospital promoted its modern and efficient management of sewage and effluent. As early as 1882 a 12-inch main took the effluent to a straining tank open to the air, half a mile to the north of the main building. The effluent was then spread, by 'gravitation' over about 2 acres of the adjoining land, but this was not a successful way of distribution and by about 1890 the land was becoming saturated. Thus In 1892 a 'new' chemical process for precipitation was introduced. This was deemed a success and this process continued until the Hospital was connected to the county sewerage system.

As a buffer between these buildings and the main road, the Hospital constructed two hard surface tennis courts. These were surrounded by trees, many of which were unusual species. Today the refurbished tennis courts are still in use and many of the trees still stand.

Even more isolated, on the north side of the road, was the sanatorium. Dating from 1890, it was a central cottage with two wings, each for four patients. Staffed by a residential matron and several nurses, this was used for the treatment of patients who had infectious diseases.

Until the recent construction of the Greenfields housing development, the lane leading to the site of this building could still be seen running alongside the site of Barnwood Builders. This lane is now the eastern part of the estate's playground.

The lane that led to the Sanatorium.

Adjacent to the sanatorium were the vegetable gardens which kept the Hospital kitchens supplied throughout the year.

Typically, the flower gardens were on the south side of the road, next to the Hospital. All of the less attractive features were on the north side.

In 1928 the electricity supply reached Barnwood, and the Hospital built a twin transformer substation to take advantage of this.

Up till then, whilst electrical wiring had been in place in many of the buildings, this was not extensive, and electricity was supplied by numerous localised generators.

The arrival of this electricity supply, coupled with much preparatory work during the preceding years, meant that all the buildings could now be supplied with mains electricity.

The kitchen gas ovens were replaced with electric ones; and new electrical kitchen equipment purchased.

The gas lighting throughout the Hospital, which had always been insufficient due to lack of pressure, was replaced with electric.

The preparatory wiring took about 6 months to complete, and a hospital electrician was hired. He lived in one of four cottages constructed in Welveland Lane.

These electrical installations were to have one more wide-ranging beneficial effect, for the Hospital was now able to purchase an electric film projector, build a projection room and show films to patients and staff alike.

Senior non-medical staff had their own houses provided by the Hospital. This was very beneficial for the Hospital paid for gas and electricity, maintained the houses and the tenants were supplied with eggs and milk from the farm. The Chief Engineer, Electrician, Head Gardener, Swineherd, Cow man, and Farm Bailiff were such people.

Some of the cottages were occupied by medical staff enabling them to easily attend when a need arose in the wards.

Satellite Properties

The Hospital was forever innovative, and it was recognised that patients often reached a stage in their treatment when, prior to discharge, they could look after themselves. The trustees also recognised for many of their patients, that it was socially more acceptable to the patients and their families that they were housed in a building that was not called a mental institution or asylum.

This concept of assisting patient to return to society was far ahead of its time, foreshadowing the activities of the National Health service some years later.

The Hospital therefore purchased several suitable buildings, both locally and also some distance from the Hospital, in which to accommodate such patients.

North Cottage (now occupied by Emmaus), the Manor House and Lynthorpe were three such local properties. Further away, the Hospital acquired Crickley Court, an old coaching inn dating from 1650 and situated at the bottom of Crickley Hill. Opened in 1938, it housed seven ladies and eventually closed about 1958. Seven Springs House was purchased at about the same time but was never used as Hospital accommodation.

Even further away, and dating from before 1672, was The Wilderness. Purchased by the Hospital sometime before 1884, it housed up to fifteen ladies. Being 900 feet above sea level, and in the Forest of Dean, it offered the Hospital ideal sanatorium conditions. It closed in 1919.

Finally, Hume Towers in Bournemouth, which was purchased in 1954 for use as a seaside holiday home. This fine building, with stained glass windows by William Morris, was situated in extensive grounds. It housed up to forty-five patients and offered a welcome respite by the seaside. It closed in 1966.

As far back as 1904, whilst the main Hospital building itself was full throughout the year the separate houses of North Cottage and the Wilderness were only partly full. It was found that the number of patients who either preferred to live there or benefitted by being there was small. There was also a preference by patients to be housed in the Hospital itself, where occupation, amusements and interests generally were more numerous and varied.

These houses were kept running for a considerable time, neither was found to be economic and both were closed in 1919, the ladies from the Wilderness were transferred to the recently converted Manor House.

In 1937 the value of separate houses was reviewed for they were then considered by the new Medical Superintendent, Dr. Fleming, as a "most essential part of modern treatment" and were to be regarded as separate nursing homes with the Hospital as a central administration.

The Lodge in Church Lane, which up to then had variously been used to house both staff and patients, was converted into a villa for three ladies, and Lynthorpe in the Barnwood Road was purchased and adapted for five gentlemen.

Including the Manor House there were now three such houses in Barnwood, all close to the main building. They were often favoured by relatives and patients who were inclined to shun any association with an 'institution'.

The acquisition of Crickley Court and then Seven Springs House soon followed, the intention being to provide additional facilities for the treatment of early mental disorder.

Crickley Court had room for seven ladies, was opened in 1938 and stayed open for the following twenty years.

Seven Springs House was a larger property with seventy-five acres of land, and on the Cotswolds a little further away. It was sold later without being used in the way intended.

A policy of establishing small subsidiary houses in the neighbourhood and at the same time carrying out broad schemes of reorganisation in the main Hospital was considered at that time to be the most logical method of applying the Hospital's resources of finance and administration.

Unfortunately, this was all brought to a halt in September 1938 with the advent of the Second World War.

Also, at this time both The Trustees and The Committee felt that there was now a deterioration in the character of the surrounding district, brought largely about by the growing development of the Gloucester Aircraft Factory at Brockworth, which they saw as encroaching into the rural area around the Hospital.

This raised the crucial question of the removal of the Hospital to another site to be actively considered. By the end of the year a decision was taken and a search for another place undertaken.

Eventually Woodchester Park and Mansion were chosen. The estate was some distance south of Barnwood in an isolated and rural setting.

Purchased in 1939, preparations were made to move the hospital there but by 1953 the venture had been abandoned and the estate sold.

The following sections describe in more detail each of these satellite properties.

The Lodge Church Lane

The Lodge.

This was constructed about 1883 as a lodge house and it was planned to house the lodgekeeper and possibly one patient there.

So far, no evidence of a drive in this area has been found, either on the ground or in maps of the time. The chapel is close by and an entrance off Church Lane to the southern part of the Hospital's grounds would have been a convenience both for this chapel and for the adjacent cricket ground. There is some evidence on one map that there was a yard alongside the Lodge which was accessed from Church Lane. This would have been where the entrance is today.

For whatever reason, it seems that The Lodge was used instead to house the newly appointed second Doctor, Dr. Soutar. He and his family lived here soon after his arrival in 1883. They moved to the main building on his appointment as Superintendent in 1892.

The building then housed three female patients, and in 1894 four male patients were housed there.

This was not the best of dwellings, for much repair work was done to it over the years. In 1899 the plumbing was improved, and the WC connected to mains drainage rather than the cesspit. In 1908 it was underpinned due to settlement. In 1921 both the Lodge and Chapel suffered subsidence due to drought and again the Lodge had to be underpinned.

In 1910 it was again occupied by the Assistant Superintendent, this time Dr Townsend.

A review of the value of separate buildings in which to care for patients took place in 1937 the value of separate houses was reviewed, and The Lodge was converted into a villa for three ladies. This arrangement continued for many years.

The Lodge was demolished in 1948 as it had been closed for some time with severe cracking in the walls.

Lynthorpe

Lynthorpe shortly before its purchase by the Hospital.

Lynthorpe was a large house on the northern side of Barnwood Road, opposite the Hospital. The building was some way back from the main road and stood on a large plot of land with a long and well-kept garden. Sometime after 1927 this became the family home of the builder, Sydney Davies.

Sydney had a strong community conscience and was a councillor for Gloucestershire. As chairman of the Gloucestershire Cricket Club, he entertained international teams at Lynthorpe. The gardens were often used for family cricket matches.

Soon after his death in June 1937 Barnwood House Hospital purchased Lynthorpe adapting it for five male patients, many of whom were given the new treatment of prefrontal leucotomy.

It is believed that Harry Fergusson, the millionaire engineer who designed the modern-day tractor was treated there.

Views of the back of the building when it was used by the Hospital.

When the Hospital closed in 1963, Lynthorpe and its grounds were purchased by the Mormon Church of Latter-Day Saints, which used the building as a church.

In 1970 a new church was erected next to Lynthorpe, and the house was demolished to provide a space for a car park.

The extensive land of this site is easily seen from the road and gives some indication of how grand Lynthorpe' s gardens must have been.

North Cottage

North Cottage was purchased by the Hospital in 1882 in order to house patients.

Opened in 1883, its 4 acres of lands were used to grow vegetables for the Hospital.

Initially it housed seven female patients. Over the years changes, improvements and alterations were made to the building. These were often requirements requested by the Commissioners in Lunacy during their annual inspection visits and mainly consisted in ensuring the building was safe for patients.

In 1892 extra windows were installed.

In 1896 the central block of the Hospital was rebuilt, depriving Dr Soutar, the Head Doctor, of his residence. During this time, he and his family lived in North Cottage.

The heating was improved in 1898 and by 1903 the building was again housing female patients. However, the reluctance of patients to be accommodated there because of their separation from the main building meant that the building was underused.

Improvements continued, in 1911, water now came from the mains supply rather than from the laundry supply.

In 1919 it eventually became the Hospital's much-needed nurses' home after an extension was built to the rear.

There was sleeping accommodation for 12, a large sitting room and a recreation room. The home was under the charge of a Matron, Miss Wyatt, who was previously Deputy at the Wilderness.

Further extensions and improvement were made during 1922-4, with the creation of 30 bedrooms, each with a basin with H&C water, and two sitting rooms.

After the closure of the Hospital, it housed nurses who worked at Coney Hill Hospital[24].

It now houses several residents as part of the Emmaus project supporting homeless people.

---

[24] Coney Hill Hospital was the County's second mental hospital which backed on to the southern boundary of the Hospital's grounds.

Wheatstone.

Sited in the grounds of the Manor Gardens, it was built in 1950 as accommodation for the Hospital's Doctors. It also housed the Hospital's Chaplain for a while.

It was tenanted then repossessed in 1976 when it was let to the Trust Secretary until September 1989.

It eventually became a cancer respite centre and part of the NHS Lymphoedema support service.

This building will be demolished and replaced with housing as part of the redevelopment of Manor Gardens.

Crickley Court

Crickley Court was at one time a Coaching Inn called "The Crown" which dates from at least 1650. This building of eight bays is sited at the bottom of the steep winding road from the Gloucester plain up to the Cotswold escarpment, its stables housed the extra horses required to pull coaches up Crickley Hill on their way to Oxford, Stow-on-the-Wold and the old Roman Road to Cirencester.

Crickley Court

The Court and lands were extensive. It had a hall, parlour, kitchen, and cellar. Adjacent was a brewhouse with chambers and rooms. There were stables, a sheep house, orchards, and a gatehouse.

The road running alongside the building is steep, relatively narrow and winding. In the late 1950s this carried all the Cotswolds traffic to and from Gloucester.

Round the property there was a long wall which lorries regularly ploughed into, requiring the maintenance staff from the Hospital to frequently go and undertake repairs.

Today there is a three-lane road to the south to take the increased and much heavier traffic. Plans are already underway for this to be enhanced and improved.

Seven Springs House

Seven Springs House

Seven Springs House was built in 1840. It is a significant property, sitting in 75 acres, at Severn Springs, not far from the Cotswold escarpment.

it was purchased by Barnwood House Hospital around 1938 as part of their desire to have a number of autonomous homes away from the Hospital. This was never used as such as it was sold soon after its purchase.

The Wilderness

The original house on this site was called Hill House and was built sometime before 1672. It was rebuilt in 1824.

Located near Mitcheldean, the site commands extensive views over the Forest of Dean and Vale of Gloucester.

Barnwood House Hospital rented this old family mansion in 1884 for a period of 8 years in order to house 15-20 convalescent patients. Initially these were lady patients, several of whom were accompanied by their 'companions'.

This was seen as a temporary residence and was often used when the fresh air up on the hilltop was considered to be beneficial to the recovery of a patient.

The trustees bought the house and its 40 acres of grounds in 1896, for the sum of £7150.

It would seem that the building needed repairs and modernisation, but for the two years after the purchase these were put on hold, because the Trustees were incurring higher than expected levels of expenditure elsewhere. But in 1899 extensive repairs, both internal and external were undertaken. New boilers and radiators were installed in 1903. Something that must have greatly pleased both staff and patients.

Like other such Barnwood House properties, patients were often reluctant to go there due to its separation from the main Hospital.

Life might have been quite primitive there for in 1911 the water supply from the well dried up, necessitating a search during the next two years for an alternative supply. This problem was triggered by the use of the building as 'holiday' accommodation for patients, who would stretch the available resources.

The Wilderness was eventually considered to be uneconomic. It was not possible to treat acute cases there, and convalescent patients preferred to be in the main building where there was more entertainment. It closed October 1919.

A story was told to me by the mechanic who retrieved the building's 'ambulance' when The Wilderness closed.
He discovered a well-established field mouse nest under the driver's seat. This vehicle had regularly been used by the matron without her realising she had passengers underneath her each time she drove it.

Woodchester Mansion

Woodchester Mansion.

Woodchester Mansion is a Grade I listed house in the Victorian Gothic style. It is absolutely unique because it is unfinished. There is a strong French influence in the style of the house which also makes Woodchester slightly different from other buildings of its type and time. It is situated at the western end of Woodchester Park, in a beautiful valley, with the village of Woodchester at the eastern end. Records of settlement in Woodchester stretch back to Roman times.

In 1935 the Mansion became the property of the Leigh family. By this time Blanche Leigh was over seventy, and she sought a purchaser for the estate. She hoped to sell to an Italian Catholic religious order who would use the Mansion, and, in particular, the chapel. Unfortunately, they were unable to raise sufficient funds and so the sale fell through.

Woodchester Park estate consisted of a mansion, two farms, cottages, and woodlands, amounting to over a thousand acres in all, but the style and nature of the mansion limited the range of potential purchasers. Nevertheless, the Hospital's Trustees were very interested in buying and were prepared to offer about £17K, far more than any other potential purchasers. A sale was agreed and, not without difficulty, possession was obtained by the close of 1939.[25]

In December 1939 Miss Leigh wrote to the Abbot of Prinknash, explaining why she had sold to the Trust. She wrote *"I told Mr Croome, Chairman of Governors, that I was not going to sell my Catholic heritage for a mess of pottage! So, he agreed to build a distinct Catholic House for not less than 20 Catholic male patients, to staff it entirely with Catholic nurses, to build, furnish and maintain a Catholic Chapel for the inmates & pay for the services of a chaplain. The building & furnishing of the Chapel is to be placed in the hands of a Catholic architect.*[26] *Our great grief is that the beautiful Chapel will now be used for non-Catholic worship; but it cannot be helped as the Mansion will not be used for patients."*

The Hospital planned to erect new buildings for the patients but use the Mansion as offices and considered Woodchester Park to be an excellent site for the needs of their patients.

The new branch quickly became established and for the eleven years of its life it provided care and treatment for a daily average of thirty-eight patients.[27]

---

[25] The Leigh family had a strong link to the Hospital, for a relative of Miss Leigh was treated there in 1907. This might have helped in the sale to a non-Catholic organisation.

[26] Whether this happened, as requested by Miss Leigh is not clear.

[27] This is from Tom Gale's history, but so far, I have not found any evidence in the records of the construction of buildings or the fitting out the mansion for patients.

The first seven years saw favourable financial results, but in the eighth and following years there were losses.

Despite the war and the restrictions upon the supply of labour and materials, work at Woodchester Park continued with the maintenance of the buildings, the farms and the young plantations and woodlands.

Between 1939-45 troops were based in the park, using the lakes in the valley to train in bridge building for the invasion of Europe after D-day. Security was high and rigorously enforced, and the Park was inaccessible. This continued after the war when visitors were discouraged, as the shooting rights were a source of income.

There were two farms, 'Longwood' of one hundred and fifty acres and 'Park' of five hundred. From 1940 Longwood was farmed from Barnwood on a commercial basis, and Park from 1948. This was not a financial success as there were difficulties of supervision from a distance and a succession of losses. A decision was taken when Park Farm came under the Hospital's management to build up the dairy herd there and a contract was made with the Milk Marketing board for the sale of milk wholesale. Extensive repairs were made to the cowsheds and farm buildings, the farmhouse was split into two dwellings and two additional cottages were built nearby, all to house farm workers. Within a year the farm had increased its supply of milk by nearly 50% and was now supplying eggs and fresh produce to the Hospital.

Looking ahead to the time of the Hospital's transfer to the new site, in 1942 the Committee purchased a property known as Bownham Park, near Minchinhampton, to provide an ancillary house for ladies within easy reach of Woodchester. This was let awaiting the move. The premises were occupied by the Soldiers' Sailors' Airmen's Families Association. They left in May 1949.

In 1949, Gravel Hill house at Bownham Park was rewired and connected to the overhead electricity supply. The cost of repairs to the estate's boundary wall was more than offset from the sale of timber from the estate. The house was still not being used for lady patients due to a shortage of staff and suitable tenants were being sought.

In the same year work was needed on the roof and walls of the Mansion. At that time, those rooms of the mansion that were habitable, a cottage and 48 acres of land were leased for use as a school.

The Trustees agreed to develop the site for the transfer of the Hospital from Barnwood. An architect of national repute was engaged, and preliminary plans were drawn in collaboration with the Board of Control. Later events rendered them abortive.

By 1953, it had become increasingly clear that the transfer of the whole Hospital from Barnwood to Woodchester, the purpose for which the Park was acquired, could never in fact be accomplished and that the farms and woodlands were not a satisfactory form of investment. Accordingly, the whole estate was sold.

The disposal of Bownham Park then became a logical outcome, and its sale, delayed until vacant possession was obtained, took place in 1955.

What the future of the Hospital would have been in this secluded valley had the plans for its transfer there materialised is pure conjecture, but with long hindsight it seems reasonable to assume that the difficulties of staffing in an isolated spot involving dependence upon part-time nurses living at a distance, together with financial and other problems, would have inevitably proved more insuperable than the problems left behind at Barnwood.

Hume Towers at Bournemouth.

Another property away from Barnwood was that of Hume Towers at Bournemouth.

The back, overlooking the gardens.

The front, from the old Manor Brochure.

Until it closed in 1954 it was a seaside branch of another institution The Old Manor, Salisbury.

At that time, many private beds had been lost because of the closing or taking over of licensed houses by Regional Hospital Boards.

The Committee decided that by purchasing Hume Towers it would serve to meet the demand for private beds and would also be a means of extending the work. It would also provide a seaside branch to which patients could be sent.

The property consisted of a large mansion, two small houses and a lodge. It was situated attractively in twelve-and- a-half acres of wooded grounds in the centre of Bournemouth.

In some ways the layout of both house and grounds mirrored that of Barnwood and it must have been an attractive proposition for the Trustees.

The Committee bought it in June 1954 and a considerable amount of repairs, improvements and reequipping were done under supervision from Barnwood.

The accommodation was for forty-five patients at a time. It was opened in the following January and by the end of the year a hundred and seventeen patients had been admitted.

It had its own medical officer and matron, but policy and central administration were derived from Barnwood.

However, the cost of maintaining Hume Towers had more often than not proved to be a burden on the resources of the Hospital.

By 1965 there was, in Bournemouth, a strong demand for building sites for private residences, so that the value of the land occupied by Hume Towers became greatly enhanced. With this in mind an application for planning permission for blocks of flats was made and obtained. The prospect of a lucrative sale was thus opened up, a purchaser was found, and a sale effected in the spring of 1966.

The Manor House

Early History of The Manor House

The Manor House was built c1740, although there do not appear to be any records for either the exact date or builder.

It was built on what was almost certainly a meadow, one of a series of plots laid out in the early 18th century along the former Roman Ermin Street.

The Inclosure map of 1799 shows the land on which The Manor House stood was leased by Mrs. Sophia Bubb from the Dean and Chapter. She also leased land on the eastern side of Upton Lane.

The naming of a plot of land to the south of the brook is interesting. Referred to as 'Jordan's 'Brook Close', this name is retained today in the name of the building on this land 'Jordan's Brook House'.

In the early days, The Manor House was the home of Samuel and Sophia Bubb who were the grandparents of the inventor Sir Charles Wheatstone, who was born in the house on 6th of February 1802.

Although Sir Charles' parents lived in the centre of Gloucester, it seems likely that his mother took up residence at her parents' house for her confinement and that this is where Charles was born. His baptism is recorded in the register of St Mary de Lode, and it may well have taken place there, as his parents lived in Westgate Street. However, there is a possibility that, as was typical of the time, the event took place in Barnwood, but the entry was made in a register which was more convenient for the minister to access. Certainly, as he grew up, the young boy spent time in Barnwood with his grandparents, for his biographer, Brian Bowers, recalls Charles talking about the house and its grounds with affection.

Around 1804 Sir Charles Hotham purchased Barnwood House. As well as buying the land immediately associated with the house, Sir Charles also purchased neighbouring properties fronting on to the Turnpike Road together with the fields between those properties and the Wotton Brook and some fields to the south of the brook. It is likely that these purchases included the Manor House and lands from the Dean and Chapter.

By 1810, the elegant symmetrical house, one room deep, had been extended with two rear wings.

In 1813, David Walters purchased this estate on the death of Sir Charles.

By now, the house was occupied by a gentleman farmer, Joseph Rea. He, and later his son, William, lived there until the latter part of the 19th century.
 In 1853 Walters died in debt and the house and land was sold once more, seemingly allowing Rea to purchase it.
Joseph Rea died shortly after in 1855, and it seems that William was responsible for the main 19th century additions to the house.
His wife Kate was a keen horticulturist and a walled garden, tennis courts and a vinery had been added.

A modern picture which clearly shows the original house on the right with the later mid-19th century addition by William Rea, on the left.

The orchards to the rear (south) of the house produced both abundant fruits of several varieties and poultry, raised within them.

William advertised frequently in the local newspaper for the sale of his poultry, raised in the orchard and also sold his fruit grown there. He kept cattle, pigs and cart horses in the adjacent stables and farm buildings to the west of the House.

The 1881 census shows William as a *'farmer of 200 Acres Employing 4 Men 3 Boys'* living at the Manor House with Kate and 2 servants.

In 1893 the Manor House estate was sold by William. It included 'Lobleys', their farm to the south of the Manor House. The sale also included the former orchard behind the house and the small orchard across the brook.

By then, the service wing of the House comprised of two kitchens and there were further offices laid around a central courtyard to the east of the house. Only the kitchens on the western end of the house remain today, the external buildings having been demolished.

The grounds included a tennis lawn and a vinery with its adjoining stove house, together with a large walled kitchen garden. Beyond the garden was a thriving orchard of fruit trees through which ran the brook. The stables and domestic farm buildings were *'at a distance from the house'* down the driveway, grouped round the former stable yard.

The Manor House ceased to be a working farmhouse with the departure of William Rea. [28]

Following the sale, the house had a series of short-term occupants: Colonel Peter Kerslake Seddon in 1894 and then in 1897 Richard Talbot, Alderman

---

[28] Much is reproduced here from the Heritage report on the Manor House by McLaughlin Ross llp (2014) commissioned by the Barnwood Trust and is used with their permission.

and High Sherriff of the City. He and his family remained there during much of the first decade.

The Talbots were commercial, owning the large Gloucester based mineral water bottling factory, and it was they who were responsible for the current main staircase. Mrs Talbot advertised continually in the local papers for domestic staff, and it is likely that they modernised the house and domestic wing.

The gardens remained primarily orchard, and it is probable that a number of specimen trees that remain today were planted by the family.

By the end of the first decade the local vicar, the Reverend Edward Roberts, had moved in, and remained there until 1913 when the house became part of Barnwood Hospital.

Bought by the Hospital

The house and grounds were purchased by the Hospital sometime after 1913 but was not always in use by the Hospital and was, at times, rented out.

In 1917 the building was offered to the War Office for use as free accommodation, with medical provision for treating officers who were suffering from shell shock; the offer was declined.

It was first used as a nursing home for the Hospital in 1919 when the Wilderness was closed, and its lady patients were transferred there.

The building could not take more than six or seven patients, and it was never run independently of the main Hospital, upon which it had to rely for a multitude of services, including considerable support financially.

The conversion of the house to a nursing home required it to be extended westward, the adjacent service buildings and small yard all being demolished to make way for this.

The Manor House was now the long rectangular building which we see today, with a wide driveway and paths all around it. The bay window was added at the eastern end and a large new chimney stack built on the garden front.

The gardens extended into the orchard, the stable yard and farm buildings to the west remained, but several glasshouses now appeared in the walled garden with an entrance through the wall into the Hospital gardens.

Physically, it remained little altered during the following years, though about 1939, in line with a change in the Hospital's policy regarding separate buildings in which to house patients, it became a nurses' home.

About 1966 it was decided to close the main Hospital but to retain the Manor House as a nursing home, initially in which to house those patients who could not be accommodated elsewhere.

The front of the Manor House when a Nursing Home.
From the Hospital's prospectus.

The details of what then happened to the Manor house may be found in the earlier section 'Continuation at The Manor House'.

The Development of the Trustees' Land

In the late 1970s, the Trust's income was modest and just sufficient to meet its obligations. This was because the revenue from its land was not great, the rents from the tenanted properties were controlled and its investment portfolio was relatively modest - some three-quarters of a million pounds.

The return of business confidence in the early 1980s coincided with the development of planning policies by Gloucester City Council affected the future use of all the Trust's land. Under these plans, part of the former farmland to the north of Barnwood Road was scheduled for commercial and industrial use, and the Trustees' land to the south of Barnwood Road, amounting to some 71 acres, was earmarked for housing development.

The eventual sale of these lands raised, in total, over £3.3m, significantly influencing the plans and future direction of the Trust's activities.

The land north of Barnwood Road still remaining in Trust ownership were the sites on Barnwood Fields leased to the Crest Hotel, Barclays Computer Centre, and the 10.5 acres adjacent to Walls factory.

The following chapters describe the sale and development of the Trust's lands and what happened to the remainder.

Residential Land

The City of Gloucester District Plan 1981 foresaw the need for a significant addition to the stock of new private sector housing to meet ever-growing local community needs over the next decade. It was proposed that a total of some 400 acres of mainly agricultural land should be used for this purpose. The projected development was referred to as 'Abbeydale III', later to be known as 'Abbeymead'.

This huge area of land, south of Barnwood Road and east of Church Lane, extended to the M5 and the existing 'Abbeydale II' development.

The Local Authority Plan envisaged the building of about 3,000 houses in a mixture of sizes and types on about three quarters of the land involved. The remaining 100 or so acres being reserved for protected sites, for public open spaces including footpaths and cycle paths, and for communal facilities of various kinds.

The sheer size of the scheme and the fact that eleven private landowners were involved, with potential rights and obligations to each other as well as to the Local Authority, resulted in the landowners and developers forming a Consortium under their own chairman.
Each had representatives, solicitors, planning consultants and architects of their own, to facilitate the expected lengthy and most complex set of negotiations with the Planning Authority over the terms for the grant of Outline Planning consent for the whole development.

The Chairman appointed by the Consortium, Charles Chivers from Bruton Knowles, was also the Trustees' adviser in all property matters. This happy coincidence ensured that the Trustees were kept fully updated with progress at all stages of the negotiations.

It was known from the outset that the Local Authority would want considerable concessions from the landowners and developers before granting outline planning consent to the development as a whole, and so it proved to be.

An idea of the difficulties encountered may be gauged from the fact that whereas outline planning consent to the Abbeydale III development was agreed in principle by the Local Authority on 27th November 1984, it was not until 27th February 1986, fifteen months later, that agreement on all the many contentious matters was finally reached, that the numerous inter-related legal documents were signed, and that Outline Planning Consent to the development was released by the Local Authority.

The reasons why it took so long to reach agreement were many and various, but huge sums of money were at stake and important principles were involved for both sides.

The Local Authority for its part had to ensure that the developers jointly bore the cost of the necessary upgrading of all the public services, and the redesign of the public road system to meet the burden of this huge development. The developers on the other hand tried to ensure that they were not being held to ransom, that is, they were not being required to fund improvements to local services in excess of that justified by the development itself.

As to the Trustees' involvement in all this, they appointed Bryant Homes, by a selection process in 1984, to develop 67½ acres of the former Barnwood Park grazing land and entered into an Option Agreement with Bryant.

The plan below shows how the Trust lands were apportioned.

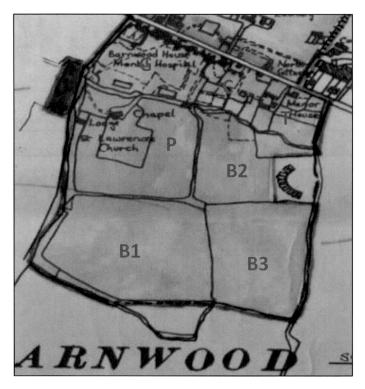

The Areas marked [G] for Grovelands, and [C] for Cherston Court are the two housing developments that resulted from the 1969 sale. Barnwood Park [P], was also as a result of this sale.

[B1], [B2] and [B3] are the three Bryant developments with [T] being the land retained by the Trust.

This Agreement provided that Bryant Homes would represent the Trustees' interests in all negotiations between the Consortium and the Local Authority, meeting all the Trustees' costs in the process, and that, after Outline Consent for the whole Scheme had been achieved, Bryant would buy from the Trustees a minimum of five acres of land a year at the full market price and would seek detailed planning consent for each tranche taken.

At the same time, the Trustees retained for their own use a parcel of some four acres of land adjoining the Wotton Brook, with access provided through the Bryant estate roads. [Annotated 'T' in the map above]. This was for 5 bungalows which were designed and built to disability standards for families with a disabled member.

Bryant Homes began building work in 1986 when the private housing market was buoyant. By September 1989 they had bought 47½ acres of the 67½ acres available to them After that, houses were becoming more difficult to sell, making the forward prospects for take-up of the remaining 20 acres more difficult to predict. [Their allocation is marked B1, B2 and B3] Eventually, the majority of the land was sold, and the housing developments completed.

Industrial Land

After the sale of the Hospital and its surrounding land, the Trust needed to consider the future of its agricultural land to the north of Barnwood Road.

A few years previously, the construction of the Barnwood bypass, which cut across the farm, gave the opportunity for the Trust to sell off part of the land to Walls' for industrial development, and now further severance by the construction of a link road brought the prospect of a new access and a change of use affecting a considerable area of the remaining land. Coupled with Gloucester City Council's planning policies for this area, this promised a substantial financial gain to the Trust.
A decision was therefore taken to stop active farming and free the land for sale or lease.

Development of the industrial land started in the late 1970s with the central 66 acres, known during development as 'Barnwood Fields'. This is the land bounded on the north by the Barnwood bypass and to the south by the properties along Barnwood Road.

The Trustees' policy at the outset was to lease rather than sell sites so as to retain the freehold interest and still achieve a worthwhile income for the benefit of the Trust

Initially market conditions were favourable to this approach and three sites were let on that basis - one to Barclays Bank (for a computer centre), one to BICC (also for a computer centre) and one to Crest Hotels.

However, from 1981 onwards the market changed, and leases went out of favour. Sites had to be sold fully serviced, that is, with all the infrastructure in place.

At this time, the Trustees were concerned that other industrial land in the vicinity would shortly be released on to the market in competition with their own. To meet this challenge and to open up the remainder of

Barnwood Fields for development, site layout plans were drawn up and received outline planning consent towards the end of 1983, conditional on the Trustees installing the roads and other public utility services at their own expense.

Undoubtedly, this project was assisted by the existing presence of the Central Electricity Generating Board on an adjoining 27½ acre site to the south which was purchased from the Trustees in 1972 and served by an access road running through the land to be developed.

The siteworks for the new development were completed in August 1984 enabling a comprehensive marketing campaign to be undertaken by Bruton Knowles, the Trustees' Property Consultants. This was directed at possible clients, identifying the sites on offer and their permitted uses.

The local planning constraints had a restricting effect on enquiries for there was a total opposition to retailing on the site. However, around 1985, Sainsburys persisted and won an appeal to build a supermarket on the site they now occupy, thus relaxing the restrictions.

The result of all this activity, at a time when business confidence was high, was that several prime frontage sites were sold between 1986 and 1988. Additional purchasers were The Cheltenham & Gloucester Building Society (now the Lloyds Bank centre); and the Imperial Life Assurance Co. of Canada (later known as Laurentian Life and today an outpost of Cheltenham's GCHQ).

Barnwood Fields swarmed with activity during 1987 and 1988 with six major sites being developed simultaneously. For a long time, the skyline was dominated by huge cranes as the main buildings were developed, and the site access roads were choc-a-bloc with earth-moving machines and lorries whilst the work proceeded.

Life returned to normal after that and by 1989 all the remaining sites had been taken up except for one of 5-acres at to the west of Sainsburys and even that was subject to an outstanding option to purchase.

Other Land

The only other land to the north of Barnwood Road owned by the Trustees were two sites severed from their other land by two public highways, the Barnwood Bypass running west/east and the A417 Link Road running north from the bypass roundabout, which is known locally as the C&G roundabout.

One of these sites, 44 acres lying north of the bypass and east of the link road, was of very poor-quality grazing land subject to partial flooding and with no easy access. It was sold to a poultry farmer in 1982.

Following the disastrous flooding in Gloucester in 2007 and the subsequent flood mitigation works, this area was developed, about 2016, into a large balancing pond with surrounding wildlife and wetlands area. Today, footpaths cross it, and access may be obtained from either side of the bypass.

The Wetlands and Balancing Pond.

The second severed site of 10½ acres, which was a long, narrow triangular shape, lay to the north of the Walls' factory site with difficult access from the busy Link Road. As Walls were not interested in taking up their option to purchase this site, it was still unsold by 1989 because of its very limited potential.

As Walls expanded, the southwestern part of this site was used for overflow parking. Eventually the south-eastern part of this site was developed for leisure purposes with the construction of a Ten Pin bowling centre, a Sports Gymnasium, and a Premier Inn Hotel with an adjoining Inn called the Wheatsheaf.

Access to the site from the link road was difficult, limited just to filter lanes, not suitable for anything more than casual, leisure use, entry being only from the south and exit only to the north.

In 1999 this plot of land and a redundant car park, previously used by Wall's employees, was developed with the construction of an Amazon Warehouse and associated groundworks.

As is the norm now in Gloucestershire, before construction could happen, an archaeological investigation of the site was undertaken. This revealed a large Roman cemetery and associated buildings in the area alongside the A417 Link Road. A watching brief in 1971 of the culverting of the Horsebere Brook as the A417 link road was constructed, evidenced the presence of a Roman burial ground and buildings in this area known as Wells Bridge. (Named after the Wells Family, who owned extensive lands in this area.) This was an area where four rights of way, possibly of some antiquity, met at a brick-built bridge crossing the Horsebere Brook. This bridge, as records show was repaired by the Hospital in 1952 and would have taken Welveland lane as it wound its way up Chosen Hill.

To improve access, traffic lights were installed, and a three-way junction constructed at the entrance to the Link Road, now allowing access from both lanes.

Welveland Lane

Welveland Lane was an important route since early mediaeval times. Dropping from the top of Chosen hill, it wound its way to its junction with Barnwood Road, where, during the 17th Century, there was a significant Coaching Inn called the Salutation. The lane would have continued southward, past St Lawrence Church, and onward to Matson.

It was the only route the Hospital had to its fields to the north. So, when the Barnwood bypass and link roads were constructed, bridges over these roads needed to be built for the movement of cattle.

Welveland lane continues along a footbridge over the A417 which has long curving steps with a small rise, suitable for the Hospital's cattle as they were driven from the farm to their grazing. This gives access to the stone bridge over the Horsebere which the Hospital had built to enable the cattle to graze on the northern part of its lands.

The lane was, and still is, a public footpath. The construction of the bypass followed by the link road created additional paths which allowed access from Barnwood into the Elmbridge area.

By the late 1970s Walls' Factory had grown significantly. It had a large number of employees but only one vehicular entrance. That was sited at the roundabout that still bears its name, at the point where Barnwood Road, the A38 into Gloucester, the dual carriageways of both Eastern Avenue and the Barnwood bypass all meet. These carriageways created an extremely busy roundabout.

There was at that time a great concern for the safety of pedestrians and cyclists around the roundabout, especially during peak times.

In 1964 Sir Thomas Rich School moved from the Centre of Gloucester to a new site at Elmbridge. This move became the catalyst for significant improvements to Welveland Lane.

Many of the pupils who attended the schools in Elmbridge and who lived in Barnwood, either walked or cycled to and from this school using this roundabout.

In the early 1980s a campaign was led by local civil engineer, Neil James to have the northern section of Welveland Lane extended and enhanced from the bypass bridge into Elmbridge. For James lived in Barnwood and his son attended Sir Thomas Rich's School.

His wish was to have a well-lit, tarmacked path suitable for both cyclists and pedestrians all the way from Barnwood Road through to the estate roads of Elmbridge.

James was successful in his venture, and still today the route is used by many pupils as they cycle between Barnwood and the school.

Recently, as development has taken place to the north of the bypass the lane's route has been altered and widened to accommodate this.

Patients

Because of its status, a high quality private mental hospital, Barnwood House attracted many patients from the upper strata of society.

For many of these, their presence there was not common knowledge, they were either not of sufficient interest to the general public, or the families ensured that knowledge of their treatment was not widely known. Admissions of well-known people were seldom common knowledge within the Hospital, and even then, a patient might be admitted under an alias.

The staff in the Hospital were extremely good at keeping "what happened in the hospital stays in the hospital".

In my interviews with ex-staff, little confidential information was forthcoming, and if there was anything, then it was to paint the background and not for publication. Confidentiality was paramount amongst the staff, and stories very rarely left the Hospital.

There are public records where patients are named.

The most comprehensive is the Lunacy Patient Admission Registers 1846-1912 which records dates of both a patient's admission and their discharge/death. The entries for these registers are only for certified patients, just indicating whether the patient was private or pauper. Entries where the patient might still be alive today are rescinded, making research into the latter part of the Hospital's patient history difficult.

For Barnwood there are some 664 entries in the available register. The Hospital's Annual Reports show a total of 1536 for this period as these would include voluntary, temporary, and certified patients.

From 1860 through to 1966 the Hospital admitted somewhat over 6,200 patients of which about 2,500 were male and 3,700 females.

Census records covering the time the Hospital was in Barnwood, do not identify patients by name, only initials and occupation. However, the 1939 Register details all the patients resident there, and as the vast majority are known to have died, their names have not been redacted. This is a most valuable source of public information.

The Hospital's Annual Reports detail the numbers of patients, discharges, and deaths for each year. They also list the conditions that were being treated and the success rate. The latter would have been very important information as it showed how successful the Hospital was, not only to the Trustees and Inspectors, but also to prospective clients who wished for a good outcome for their family member.

The Hospital was for ever keen to ensure that a patient could be successfully treated and eventually discharged. For instance, in 1888, three patients were successfully discharged after being in the Hospital for some 10 years.

Types of Illnesses

In the early days the recognised mental disorders were divided into two sections, either moral or physical.

The report of 1880 is somewhat revealing of the thinking of the time. Those symptoms seen as being due to a moral cause were: - Pecuniary Reverse (Bankruptcy), Domestic Affliction (Possibly a euphemism for the menstrual cycle and associated gynaecological problems), and Intemperance (Alcoholism).

Whilst symptoms associated with Physical causes were: - Eczema, Overwork, Brain Disease, Puerperal (Post Natal), and Injury to the head. The majority of cases recorded that year were classified as being hereditary.

Later, these symptoms were expanded to include: - GPI (General Paralysis of the Insane) the result of syphilis, Melancholia, female "distress", Idiocy, epilepsy ("seizures"), shellshock (post WWI), "delusions" (paranoia), mania, "violently aggressive", moral failings and dementia.

However, by 1900 the understanding of the causes had developed, and the categorisation of a patient's condition was based now more on their symptoms and how the patient presented.

For the year 1880, the records show that the majority of the Hospital's patients were suffering either with 'chronic mania', 'melancholia' or 'dementia'.

Over the years, in the Annual Reports, the Head Doctor often commented on the mental disorders of patients being admitted and how the success rate of cure was influenced by the initial condition of these patients.

In 1892 Dr Soutar complained that the delay in admitting patients, often meant that they were incurable. So, by 1894, there was a significant change in the philosophy of patient admission, the chronically insane with no hope of cure were no longer being cared for and those patients removed from the Hospital so that acute cases could be admitted, treated, and discharged in a relatively short time. This is again reported by Dr. Soutar in 1898 when he says 'that we have patients without any prospect of recovery. Dementia being the most common affliction.' The Hospital was again taking steps to reduce these numbers so that those who would recover could be admitted.

Two years later he continues to comment on the type of patient that the Hospital should accept, explaining that "voluntary patients often do not benefit from being in an asylum as they often need different treatment." He refers to "unnecessary placement by friends and relatives". These are patients who can make a rational judgement about their future and whose friends and families bring them for admission. Typical would be the elderly, those who were a nuisance to the family and those women who had given birth to an illegitimate child.

This continuing policy of discharging patients who were incurable and only accepting those who would benefit from the buildings and their surroundings, resulted in the numbers of long-term patients dropping from a high of 161 in 1892.

The changes in admission policy to only accept patients 'who have a reasonable chance of recovery, where their affliction is seen as temporary and may be cured by treatment' was justified by Dr. Soutar when he commented that "the accommodation and facilities are costly and would be unproductive if the patients could not derive benefit from them".

About 70% of patients discharged are cured. The remainder are transferred to other institutions. (In line with the policy of not keeping incurable patients.)

He comments that there are several patients who "had become attached to the Hospital and are elderly".

Dr. Soutar discusses the causes of insanity and concludes that some 55% is inherited or genetic. Melancholia/depression is now more prevalent than mania.

In 1916, he commented about how many deaths were of aged patients who had been with the Hospital for many years. The average age of six of these was 84.

By 1935 The Hospital still had a large number of patients whose conditions were incurable, notably dementia, some 84 – just over half the residents. Though the numbers being admitted with these conditions were small, these patients tended to stay for a long time.

From about 1939, when a change in legislation meant that admission rules changed, the patient's family or sponsor, had to fill in a detailed admission card detailing the patient's history. The Hospital was now in a far better position to assess and treat a patient.

On admission, the patient would be given a warm bath and a full medical examination.

Their possessions would be recorded in the 'Patient Property Book' and those of any significance or value would be taken for safe keeping.

This book gives an interesting insight into the type of patient admitted, for in the early days there are many mentions of 'gold-coloured watches' (the staff were not jewellers so could not verify that the item was more than golden in colour), jewellery, fountain pens and even in one case a pistol. However, towards the end there are fewer entries, the final one recording that the patient had a plastic purse. Perhaps this reflects that the wealthy were now going elsewhere or that those admitting patients ensured that they did not come with valuables.

The Hospital had its own X-ray equipment and there was also a dentist's chair.

Patients might be admitted from another hospital and so case notes would accompany them.

The Hospital was there to treat mental conditions, not physical, though it could call on outside resources when needed. It had consultants available, these included visiting Physicians, a Surgeon, Pathologist, and a Dentist. Available were other specialists including a Gynaecologist, Radiologist, Chiropractor, Throat Nose and Ear Surgeon, Orthopaedic Surgeon, Neurological Surgeon, and an Anaesthetist.

The Hospital was always at pains to promote how successful it was. Patients would leave their care categorised as 'Recovered', 'Relieved' or 'Not improved'. Some of the latter might be transferred to other hospitals. These might be the elderly whose likelihood of a cure was remote and whose place in the Hospital was better used by someone whose chance of recovery was good.

Suicides

Although not common, suicides were not unknown. In 1884 the Head Doctor comments in the Annual Report for that year that there were a high proportion of patients suffering from melancholia and suicidal tendencies.

Those patients who exhibited suicidal tendencies were constantly monitored day and night but as one inquest recorded, a moment's lack of attention on the part of the staff would be rapidly seized upon by patients intent on ending their lives. In this case a lady patient strangled herself by escaping and hiding herself in a toilet whilst being accompanied down some stairs. The nurse had not realised the patient was not with her until it was too late. The coroner was critical of the nurse and Hospital at the inquest.

Another example of the extremes patients would go to occurred in 1882, when a male patient, resident on the 3rd floor of the main building, threw a case through the wrought iron bars of his bedroom window and followed it out landing on ground 30 feet below. He made a full recovery but cracked 3 ribs. His attendant was in room next door but could not prevent this attempt at suicide.

A tale of another suicide was related to the author by a former member of staff who was getting married and therefore had to seek employment elsewhere. Whilst on duty as a domestic, barely two hours before being interviewed in Gloucester for her new job, she discovered a lady patient hanging in a cupboard.

Despite the shock she still attended the interview, where she discovered that one of her interviewers was the husband of the lady who had just committed suicide.

It is an interesting reflection that she was not offered counselling or support as would be done today.

The pond at the bottom of the grounds, through which the brook ran, was a place where patients tried to drown themselves. This was never successful for it was not deep. Such a patient would be rescued and removed, wet and very muddy.

But patients did not always use the Hospital. Many patients were seen as a low risk and a given the freedom to leave the Hospital. Especially those ladies in North Cottage, who were being prepared for their return to society. In 1903 such a patient committed suicide on the nearby railway line as she felt unworthy to return to society.

in 1902, one suicidal female patient escaped and drowned in a reservoir several miles from the Hospital. She was just 38 and had been a patient for 6 months.

Escapes

In the early days the Hospital's grounds were surrounded either by wooden fencing or hedgerows which gave a non-restrictive feel to the area.

It was some while before the boundary wall along Church Lane was constructed. This was 'more to keep people out rather than the patients in'. The northern, Barnwood Road, boundary eventually had a brick wall all the way along it, with just the one access leading to the Hospital building's main entrance, which was monitored at all times.

The eastern boundary initially, was the wall between Manor House and the Hospital grounds, and when the Hospital purchased The Manor and its grounds, the wall along Upton Lane served as its eastern boundary.

It seems that the southern boundary to the Hospital's grounds remained either open or was a line of trees and hedgerows. Initially, the fields southward from this boundary stretched to Upton St Leonards and Matson. Even when Coney Hill Hospital was built on these fields, it was still possible to walk, unrestricted, from Barnwood House out into the country.

The Hospital's rule book clearly stated that if an attendant was negligent and a patient escaped, the cost of capturing and returning the patient would be taken from their wages.

Such was the professionalism of the staff that when one male patient offered his attendant a 'year's salary' to be allowed to escape, this tempting offer was declined. Apparently, the patient could well afford this bribe.

However, this was not always the case for in 1901 one attendant was given a months' notice for allowing a patient to escape.

Like suicides, escapees were often very determined in their actions. Here are some examples from the Annual Reports.

In 1898 two ladies escaped, one was returned within the hour, the other was returned five days later from another hospital which she 'preferred to Barnwood'.

One male escaped after visiting a church and locking the Doctor accompanying him inside. The patient made his escape and went abroad!

1905 saw three patients escaping, two were returned within 12 hours the other, a gentleman was missing for 15 days before turning up at his friends.

An interesting report in the Annual Report of 1916, describes how one patient, a South African, who did not speak English, escaped. He was captured by the police and detained as an unregistered alien for several days until his identity was established, then returned to the Hospital.

Some patients, especially those who were well on the way to recovery, were free to wander the grounds and surrounding roads. A true story is one of a male patient who had wandered across Barnwood Road and entered the Engineer's Cottage. It was mid-afternoon, and the engineer was sitting quietly in the kitchen having a cup of tea. Being sociable and realising the man was not a threat, a cup of tea was offered and the two sat convivially chatting, passing the time. A quiet phone call into the Hospital to Male No.1 Ward resulted in the eventual appearance of one of the attendants and the patient was quietly returned to the Hospital. About a year later a letter arrived at the Engineer's Cottage. Posted in America it contained a thank you note 'for a most enjoyable afternoon chatting over a cup of tea'. The signature on the letter was that of a well-known and very wealthy American gentleman.

Deaths

Whilst the Hospital's main aim was the cure of patients, it was recognised early on that it also had a role in caring for those patients who would never be able to return to society, many of whom would spend the rest of their lives in their care.

Apart from death by natural causes, there were those patients who would die possibly as a result of their mental illness or of an illness that affected their mental condition.

A death could be due to an underlying medical problem which was not causing their mental condition and might not have occurred if the patient had been treated in a general hospital. Many of the patients were unable to clearly communicate their symptoms and so these could have been missed by the staff whose specialities were mental not physiological.

Influenza swept through the Hospital several times, resulting in the premature deaths of many patients.

An analysis of the Hospital records shows that over its time in Barnwood, some 21% of the admissions died. Reflecting, possibly, the high number of elderly patients it cared for. In some years the deaths were few, in others, high. The most common number per year was about 32. In total there were some 1300 deaths during the 108 years the Hospital treated patients in Barnwood. About one quarter of these deaths are buried in the graveyard of nearby St Lawrence Church. These have been identified from the burial registers as their abode was 'Barnwood House'.

The costs of maintaining a patient

Patients were charged according to their means, so those who could afford it were charged more than those who could not.

The Hospital was very mindful of its obligation to supplement the payments of those patients who stood 'a reasonable chance of recovery' but did not have the means to pay. However, the terms of its charity prohibited the Hospital to subsidise the treatment of a patient who did not show a this.

The following are examples of the annual costs of maintaining and treating a patient and the fees paid to the Hospital for this.

Whilst in the early years the Hospital made a comfortable profit, in its latter years this dropped, and by 1966, just before it closed, it was making a loss.

Although a patient paid for their basic care, there were 'incidentals' such as laundry, trips out, and sometimes additional medication and consultancy.

In the early days, the annual income from the patients was somewhat over £12,500, with expenditure of about £10,000, giving a comfortable surplus, and by 1900 the income had risen to £24,000 giving 27% surplus.

Expenditure and income rapidly increased after this time but by 1935, even with an income of £44,000, there was now only a small surplus as expenditure had risen to £41,000.

In today's money this is about £3 million. Then, a patient was paying about £5 11s. per week, which would have been equivalent to about £400 in today's money.

By 1966 the Hospital was making a loss with an income of £124,000 against £139,000 expenditure. Correspondingly the patient charges per week were £19, but expenditure costs were £21 per week per patient.

Many patients were charged several guineas per week, whilst many others just paid the going rate, and for some the cost of treatment was greater than for others, so the figures are an average.

Patient Demographics

Whilst Census records do not name patients, they do indicate their 'occupation'.

For the female patients there was a predominance, some 90%, who were 'living on their own means' or similar. It was unusual to see other occupations other than 'wife'. Though in 1939 the Hospital was looking after four teachers, one student and a medical practitioner.

For the males the majority were again 'private means' but a much smaller percentage, about one third. At any one time there would be several students, farmers, teachers, and clerics in the Hospital, whilst the rest of the male patients came from a professional background.

The Patients

The following stories typify some of the patients the Hospital looked after.

There are strict restrictions on what can be written about the patients the Hospital treated. I have therefore only used names where there is public record of the person being there and sought to make all other information anonymous.

The story of a female patient

This section contains details of a patient's conditions that some readers might find distressing.

Whilst looking through the patient names in the 1939 Register, an unusual name caught my eye. Some research confirmed that this was a lady law student, not a common occupation for a lady at that time. Permissions were sought and obtained to look at her medical records and after contacting her family, they have allowed me to reproduce them here, removing any information that might identify her. They show how a female patient might be admitted, what her symptoms were, her treatment and her eventual death in the Hospital.

She was first admitted, as a Voluntary Patient, to an Asylum on 24th of October 1930 [aged 20+].

The onset of her affliction was when she was aged 20 years and 8 months, just before her admission.

Eighteen months later in July 1932, she was made a Temporary Patient by order of the Board of Control. This was the official body that oversaw private asylums and their patients

She was subsequently transferred to Barnwood and admitted as a Temporary Patient on 2nd of August 1932.

The medical notes that accompanied her referred to 'her erratic and peculiar conduct for about 18 months'. They stated that 'she had an unfortunate low opinion and had failed in several examinations. She had hoped to become a barrister.

Accompanying her notes was a letter from the matron giving more details about the patient's condition. 'She speaks with a very low voice, which is scarcely audible, and fixes her eyes on one spot. She said she had killed all her family and that she was very wicked. She refuses her food as she thinks that the nurses are starving, and she was taking food from them.

She speaks in a low monotone and keeps her eyes fixed in one corner of the room. She does not think she should eat as she was so wicked, and that the spirit voices had told her that she was. She also said that the voices had told her to kill herself.'

On arrival at Barnwood, she was given a warm bath and examined. She had an abrasion on her back and an old operation scar on the abdomen.

Throughout August the Barnwood notes comment on her refusal to take food, her confused state, and her inability to hold an intelligible conversation.

She had a violent outburst on the 12th of September and had to be sedated.

There was not much change in her condition during the following months, but on the 26th of December the entry in her notes records that she has been subject to impulsive outbursts for no apparent reason, and that she is undoubtedly a case of Catatonia Dementia Phaerux

Her term of being a Temporary patient came to an end and so she was certified. This was done on 28th of December. The certificate stated, 'She sits in a constrained attitude with her head thrown back and eyes tightly shut.' 'She mutters incoherently and giggles all the time.' She talks in a quiet manner but is incapable to say what the conversation is about.'

She was aged just 22. And is recorded as a 'Law Student'. The guarantor of the 5 guineas per week fee was her brother-in-law.

During the following years the staff observed very little change in her condition, though it was noted that after a holiday in Weston-Super-Mare she looked somewhat better.

During the early part of 1945 the staff were becoming concerned that she had an intestinal problem, but tests were inconclusive. The entries in her records increase during March, the staff are obviously aware she is not well and suspect a problem either with her lungs or digestive system.

On the 30th of March she became unconscious about 5pm and died at 10:20pm. She was aged 35.

A post-mortem was carried out the following day. A thrombosis was discovered in her small intestine. The death certificate from the Hospital gave the cause for death as Mesenteric Thrombosis. Mesenteric venous thrombosis occurs when a blood clot forms in one or more of the major veins that drain blood from your intestines. This condition is rare, but it can lead to life-threatening complications without prompt treatment.

Stories of some of the male patients

Joseph

His name caught my eye whilst looking for Barnwood patients in the Lunacy Patient Admission Registers. Here there were several entries for him, ending up at Barnwood. His story shows how patients were often moved from institution to institution before ending up at Barnwood.

Joseph was born in 1832 and was a watchmaker. He was admitted to Burman Hospital in Henley in Arden on the 24th of May 1864, aged 32. Five years later he was discharged on the 21st of July 1869 his condition was stated as 'not improved'. That day he went from there to Droitwich Lunatic Asylum where he stayed for two years being discharged on the 10th of Sept 1871, when he went to Barnwood, again 'not improved'. There he was admitted aged 38, to ward M3, indicating that he needed constant care. The diagnosis of Joseph's condition was dementia, which he had been suffering from since the age of 21.

The fees were recorded as £100 annually, indicating that his stay was anticipated to be many years, borne out by the fact that he lived there for another 45 years.

He died of senile decay and cerebral haemorrhage, on the 24th of April 1916, aged 84, and is buried in the graveyard of St Lawrence, Barnwood. Here we have a patient who spent over half his life in mental institutions, the majority of which was in Barnwood.

For each patient the Hospital required some form of guarantee for the fees. In Joseph's case, there were two guarantors. Whether the annual payment, initially of £100, was met for all the 45 years and where this came from can only be surmised.

However, a patient who was of a different status was a retired Cheltenham schoolmaster, who, aged, 58 was admitted to Barnwood by his family in November 1914. His fees were 36 guineas per week which would have meant private bedroom and possibly a servant.

He was diagnosed with melancholia, which was determined to be hereditary. He had financial worries and was considered suicidal. He died there in January 1941.

Another patient who was charged a goodly fee, 6 guineas per week, was a civil servant aged 77. He was admitted to the Hospital on the 17th of July 1938 and died there a week later of bronchial pneumonia.

Thomas was a patient who is buried alone in the Barnwood churchyard and whose life is tinged with sadness and some mystery.

Born in 1825, Thomas decided to enter the medical profession and was, at the age of 23, awarded his certificate to practice on 27th April 1848.

By 1881 he was boarding in London, but no longer practicing as a surgeon, even though he was only 56 years of age.

Four years later, at the age of 60, Thomas married a widow at the parish church Brimpsfield on the first of December 1885. This was his first marriage. Her second, her husband having died some years earlier.

A bout of insanity seized him just one month after his marriage, when he was convinced that he was unable to pay his debts and was being chased by creditors. He spent some time in the Brooke House Asylum in Hackney. This was the area he had lived in for some years previously.

In the light of what was to follow, it is interesting to note that there are two records of him discharging himself from the Hackney Workhouse in August and September 1868

Six months later, on 28th of June 1886, whilst living at Churchdown, Thomas has another episode and was admitted to Barnwood House Hospital. He is described as "a little, feeble, broken down, twittering man". He has no teeth, "his face is emaciated, he looks haggard and exhausted, and his general expression is one of blank stupor and absolute mental paralysis". His admission notes make sad reading, and it is clear from them that he has suffered from Syphilis as well as 'Brain Disease'.

It would seem that Thomas had led an intemperate life and this spell of illness, which caused his admission to Barnwood House followed from an excessive bout of drinking. He spent his days wandering and muttering to himself and had to be fed via a stomach pump.

Thomas died on the 6th of September 1886 from "Brain disease and exhaustion", although we would now recognise this as dementia.

When his widow died in 1897, she was clearly a reasonably well-off lady as she left numerous gifts of money, including legacies to The General Infirmary and the Gloucestershire Eye Institution. She further directed that she should be buried in the brick grave in Hempstead churchyard which held the body of her previous husband.

An edited version of 'Who's who in the churchyard' by John Williams.

Notable patients.

Several well-known patients who were looked after by the Hospital have this fact recorded in the public domain. Here are just a few.

Sir Fabian Ware

Major-General Sir Fabian Arthur Goulstone Ware was a British educator, journalist, and the founder of the Imperial War Graves Commission, now the Commonwealth War Graves Commission.

In April 1949, he was taken ill at his home in Amberly. The symptoms were diagnosed as being a mental disorder and he was taken to Barnwood House Hospital.

On admission the staff realised that the symptoms were due to a heart attack, and he died soon after.

Henry (Harry) Ferguson

Henry George Ferguson was born 4th of November 1884, in County Down, Ireland.

Ferguson had been suffering from depression and was admitted to Barnwood House Hospital on the 30th of August 1958. He left there on 18th of October but was readmitted on 30th of that month but was discharged the following day.

He died on the 25th of October 1960 (aged 75) at Stow-on-the-Wold, Gloucestershire.

Hi death was the result of a barbiturate overdose. However, the inquest on his death was unable to conclude whether this had been accidental or not.

It is said that Ferguson spent some time in Lynthorpe. It was here that male patients recovered before being allowed home.

Kitty Armstrong

She was a patient in the Hospital who though not notable in herself, her husband became notable after her death.

Herbert Armstrong was a 53-yearold solicitor in picturesque Hay-on-Wye. He was also a retired Territorial Army Major. A small mild-mannered man who, it is said had married a domineering woman who nagged him continuously.

His wife, Katherine, was a hypochondriac, who was frequently ill. Her husband, kept in close contact with her doctor, Dr Hincks, and showed great concern for his wife, often consulting relatives and friends.

Hincks found that Mrs Armstrong was showing signs of mental collapse and concluded that it was connected to her illness. She was certified insane in July 1920 and at the end of August of that year, Mrs Armstrong was admitted to Barnwood Hospital.

On admission she had pyrexia, vomiting, heart murmurs, and albumen in the urine. There was also partial paralysis in the hands and feet and loss of muscle tone. Mrs Armstrong was also delusional.

Her condition began to improve at Barnwood, and she was discharged home on 22nd January 1921.

Shortly after her return home her condition mysteriously deteriorated again, and she died of an agonising illness exactly a month after her return on 22nd February.

Her death was certified as gastritis by a doctor, Armstrong then went on a long holiday to recover from the ordeal.

The story of Kitty Armstrong might have ended there but for events that were to subsequently unfold.

Another solicitor in Hay-on-Wye was Mr. Oswald Martin. He was in dispute with Armstrong professionally. Armstrong invited Martin to tea where he handed Martin a scone, apologising, "Excuse fingers." Later that day Martin was violently ill and his father-in-law, who was also the town's chemist, informed the doctor treating Martin that Armstrong had made several purchases of arsenic. The doctor agreed to send a sample of Martin's urine for analysis and, as suspected, it proved to contain quantities of arsenic.

On the 31st of December 1921 Armstrong was arrested and charged with the attempted murder of Oswald Martin.

Mrs Armstrong's body was then exhumed and Bernard Spilsbury, the famous pathologist, carried out a post-mortem. It contained two hundred and eight milligrams of arsenic. Though the body had been buried for ten months it was in a remarkable state of preservation, this being due to the mummifying effect of the arsenic.

On the 3rd of April 1922, Armstrong was tried at Hereford for the murder of his wife. The trial is notable for the weight of medical evidence.

It seems that staff at Barnwood were suspicious that Kitty became unwell soon after eating chocolates sent to her anonymously. These were examined by the Hospital staff and found to contain arsenic. Needless to say, she improved when these were withheld from her. Why this was not followed up with the authorities is not clear, though there may not have been sufficient evidence for an investigation.

Although Barnwood's Head Doctor, Greig Soutar had retired and left Barnwood, he was called to give evidence at the trial of Armstrong.

Armstrong was found guilty and went to the gallows at Gloucester Prison on the 31st of May 1922, where John Ellis and Edward Taylor hanged him.

Herbert Armstrong was the only solicitor in the history of the United Kingdom to have been hanged for murder.

Hon. Hersey Annabelle Drummond

Hon. Hersey Annabelle Drummond was the daughter of William Henry Drummond, 7th Viscount Strathallan, a Lord in waiting to Queen Victoria in 1859.

Born in Perthshire in 1846, she was admitted to Barnwood on the 16th of June 1879, aged 33 years. It is not known why, though in May 1899 her medical records stated she that had chronic mania and excitement.

When she was admitted, the Hospital had only been operating for 19 years, but by then it had established itself and had a good reputation. This may have been why her family sent her there.

The patient's property book records that, on admission, she had with her a silver cross and chain, 2 broches, sundry beads and chains, a gold bangle, a gold locket, gold earrings, lorgnettes, a broken gold watch, 2 silver chains, a silver bracelet, a coral pin, and 4 gold rings.

Last of all she had a chatelaine. This is a decorative belt, hook, or clasp worn at the waist with a series of chains suspended from it. Each chain is mounted with useful household appendages such as scissors, thimbles, watches, keys, vinaigrette, and household seals.

She died on 23rd of February 1939, aged 92 and was buried in St. Lawrence Churchyard, Barnwood.

Aged 33 on admission, she had been a patient there for sixty years.

In the British Newspaper Archives for 1939, there is no record of Hersey's funeral. It is possible that the family wanted to keep her 'lunacy' quiet or by then contact with the family had been lost.

Hersey Drummond's grave in Barnwood Churchyard

In the annual reports of the 1920s the head doctor complained of the numbers of patients that are incurable and should not be keeping places that other, curable, patients could use.

Hersey could have been one of the patients he was referring to. Keeping her there was maybe the only option. She would possibly have been paying the upper level of fees and funding the other, less profitable patients. The presence there of an 'Hon Lady' might also have been seen as beneficial for the promotion of the Hospital.

There is one image of her in the National Portrait Gallery which was made when she was about 21 and which was bequeathed to them by Francis Needham in 1971. Probably the son of Frederick Needham who was Barnwood's Superintendent between 1874 and 1892 and if so, it could be assumed that this picture accompanied her throughout her time at Barnwood.

Ivor Gurney

One notable patient to be treated by the Hospital was Ivor Gurney, the well-known Gloucester poet and musician who suffered mentally after his return from serving in the First world War.

Medical help was sought for him, but to no avail and on the 28th of September 1922, Gurney was certified insane and admitted to Barnwood House Hospital.

Here he began to write the first of dozens of letters of appeal to the great and the good, to the police, to universities, and to friends and colleagues, crying out for release or death. He encapsulated his thoughts in a poem he wrote whilst there called 'To God' crying out for release or death.

One symptom of his illness was his paranoia that electricity was affecting his brain. (This was some years before the development of the Electro Convulsive Therapy treatment that was developed at Barnwood and was used to treat patients by applying electric shocks to the brain.)

He made a desperate night-time escape, smashing a window, cutting his hands in the attempt, and running off in his pyjamas.

He was recaptured by the police, but it was then decided that he must be confined somewhere well away from Gloucestershire and so with the help of Marion Scott and other London friends, including Vaughan Williams, Walter de la Mare and Arthur Benjamin, arrangements were made to transfer Ivor to the City of London Mental Hospital at Dartford in Kent.

'Spike' Milligan

Lastly, one person that is thought to have been a patient in Barnwood is the actor and comedian Spike Milligan. I have looked for evidence of his admission to Barnwood, and so far, have found none.

A biography of Spike, written by Humphry Carpenter in 2003, describes him having mental episodes requiring his first hospitalisation at St Luke's Psychiatric Hospital at Highgate, London in 1952 (page 137). There is no reference in this biography to hospitalisation in Barnwood.

If, however, as current hearsay has it, he was in Barnwood, it must have been after 1952, and for a brief and un-reportable time.

The Hospital was happy to have short-term patients, whose condition could be overcome by being in a pleasant and high-quality environment.

There is no record of anyone with the surname Milligan in either of the Barnwood or Hume towers Superintendent's Registers, so it seems unlikely that if he was admitted it was either unrecorded in these registers or he did not use his own name.

Into the Twenty First Century

At the turn of the century both of the Trust's ventures in Barnwood, the Day Care Centre and Sheltered Housing, were well established and providing a much-appreciated service to the community.

The housing was full, or nearly so, and with its residential warden and two deputy wardens supplying 24hr cover, this was seen as a successful enterprise.

The daily stream of small coaches ferrying clients to and from the Day Care Centre equally attested to the success of this facility.

However, in a similar way to that which had affected the Hospital many years previously, the Trust were to be faced with changing circumstances.

Changes in the legislation covering sheltered housing forced the Trust to evaluate their role as a trust.

One result of the changes was that no longer was it possible to supply 24hour cover from the wardens.

Eventually the management of the Sheltered Housing was handed over to Elim Housing Association, a specialist organisation, and the Day Care Centre wound down.

The Trust's administration and offices were still based in The Manor House, but as their vision grew, so did staff numbers, and by 2010 the Trusts activities were being managed from Ullenwood Manor Farm on the edge of the Cotswold escarpment overlooking Gloucester.

The Manor House was then closed, awaiting a decision on its future.

At this time the Trust started to recruit 'Community Builders' offering support to the wider Gloucestershire community. The Trust also changed its name to 'Barnwood Trust' reflecting its change in focus.

Eventually, a larger and more central premises became essential, and The Barnwood Trust converted Overton House, a property they owned in the centre of Cheltenham, not only for their now significant workforce, but also as a purpose-built centre to support their increasing work across Gloucestershire.

This four-storey house had previously been leased to the National Star College for student accommodation, and after a £4 million renovation project to overhaul the structure of the building and improve accessibility, the new base for The Trust's work across the county, was opened in Autumn 2019.

Overton House.

In 2014 the Trust commissioned a Heritage report on The Manor House and grounds as it considered what to do with the site.

By the late 2019 decisions had been made as to how best to utilise Manor Gardens and so in early 2020 the Trust obtained planning permission to redevelop the site.

The phase 2 sheltered housing scheme of now outdated one-bedroom bungalows would be demolished and replaced with 44 new, accessible, apartments and family homes.

Two new bungalows would be built across the Wotton Brook on their adjacent Newstead Road site to supplement those already there. In addition, the Manor House would be refurbished to complement the site.

Following the impact of Covid-19 on the Trust's resources and rising costs of the project, Barnwood Trust had a change of strategy, and began a search for a suitable housing provider to take ownership. Stonewater Developments were appointed in 2022.

The new scheme remained basically as envisioned by the Trust, but Stonewater applied to convert the Manor House into a community space, offices and four apartments, two of which would be fully accessible.

Elim Housing Association stepped down as the Trust's managing agent at Manor Gardens. This is following more than 10 years of skilled, dedicated, and resident focused service at the scheme, by Elim.

And so, in 2022, after 162 years, The Trust's involvement in Barnwood came to an end.

What is left now of Barnwood House Hospital are memories, some buildings and its legacy lying here between the pages of this book.

Acknowledgements

Where I have quoted from published documents, this is credited in the footnotes.

All efforts have been made to establish and acknowledge the copyright of pictures used in this publication. If I have failed to correctly attribute this, my apologies. Please notify me and I will make suitable corrections.

Pictures on pages 71, 75, 87, 147, 151, 157, 166, 168, 169, 170, 191, and 194 are copyright Richard Auckland.

Pictures on pages 12, 13, 14 and 26 are from the publication 'Horton Road and Coney Hill Hospital' by Ian Hollingsbee and are used with his permission.

The pictures on pages 111, 112 and 113 are Copyright the Estate of W. Ross Ashby and are used with their permission.

Thanks to Jill Tucker for her picture on page 117 of the administration staff, and her recollections of her time in the administration team of the Hospital.

The image of the Drummond gravestone on page 235, is by Alison Grey and used with her permission.

The picture on page 108 of Jack Bishop and a patient is from the members of his family.

The picture from the Citizen newspaper, on page 136, was previously used in 'More Tales of Old Barnwood' with their permission.

The picture of Lynthorpe on page 164 is used with kind permission of Fay Fisher.

The aerial view of the hospital on page 151 is from the Barnwood Local History Facebook group and is used with the permission of David Taylor.

The pictures of Italian cooks on pages, 127, 131, and 132 are used with the permission of Lesley Iwaseek.

The picture of Henry Baldwin is from Marie Baldwin and used with her permission.

Robin Morris has given permission for the use of his pictures of the House. The two additional pictures, on pages 57 and 64 are from Trish Gage.

An annotated map of Manor Gardens on page 79 is used with the permission of McLaughlin Ross llp (2014).

The picture on page 66 of the final demolition is from Sheila Morgan.

The picture of Woodchester Mansion is used with the permission of Liz Davenport from the Woodchester Mansion Trust.

The annotated map on page 18 is from Gloucestershire Archives ref: Q/SRh/1810/1

The remaining pictures are from the Barnwood House deposition D3725 at the Gloucestershire Archives and are used with the permission of both Gloucestershire Archives and the Barnwood Trust.

In addition, I would like to thank the following for their contributions to my research: -

Members of Selwyn School Facebook Group who shared their memories of their time living in Barnwood.

Robin Morris for his memories and pictures of the house and grounds he occupied after the Hospital was sold.

My thanks also go to the following for their permissions to use their material.

John Williams for permission to use his articles on 'Patrick' and Fabian Ware and his help with research on the Honourable Hersey Drummond.

Gordon Owen for sight of the deeds of his property and for allowing me to take photographs from his house.

Peter Whittingham for clarification on the final sale in 2000.

Byron Hadley for his research and assistance with some of the records in D3725.

Ian Hollingsbee for permission to use images and text from his book on Horton Road and Coney Hill Hospital.

Liz Davenport from the Woodchester Mansion Trust for permissions to use text from their web site and additional background material.

I would especially like to acknowledge the support and advice from the staff at Gloucestershire Records Office. This has been a long project, requiring many hours of research in their reading room.

Lastly, my very grateful thanks go to Barnwood Trust for not only supporting me in this project with the necessary permissions and authorisations to delve through the 144 boxes of the Hospital's archive material but also supporting me financially in the production of this book.

And finally

To Eryl Copp, Nina Hargrave, and Brian McBurnie go my thanks for their proofreading, editing and advice.

Most importantly, my grateful thanks go to my longsuffering wife, Di, who not only patiently endured many days, weeks, months, and years when I spent hours muttering in front of a computer screen, but read and corrected the final text, tactfully correcting and suggesting changes.

It is to her, with all my love, that I dedicate this book.